STAR WARS:

FROM CONCEPT TO SCREEN TO COLLECTIBLE

STAR WARS:

······ FROM ····▶ CONCEPT ········▶ TO ········▶ SCREEN ·········▶ TO ·········▶ COLLECTIBLE

BY STEPHEN J. SANSWEET

PRINCIPAL PHOTOGRAPHY BY STEVE ESSIG

ADDITIONAL PHOTOS BY DAVID TUCKER

CHRONICLE BOOKS · SAN FRANCISCO

Dedicated to

Bob Canning,

for sharing the adventure,

to

Eimei Takeda and Tom Nelson,

true friends in the Force,

and to

Obi, the "other"

Copyright © and trademark ™ 1992
by Lucasfilm Ltd.

Manufactured in China

Library of Congress Cataloging-in-Publication Data
Sansweet, Stephen J. 1945–
Title: Star Wars: From Concept to Screen to Collectible
by Stephen J. Sansweet
p. cm
Includes bibliographical references.
ISBN 0-8118-0101-2. — ISBN 0-8118-0096-2 (pbk.)
1. Star Wars films—History and criticism.
2. Star Wars films—Collectibles. I. Title
PN1995.9.S695S26 1992
791.43'75—dc20   91-44507
CIP

Graphic Design: Earl Gee & Fani Chung
Earl Gee Design, San Francisco
Typesetting: Z Prepress

Distributed in Canada by Raincoast Books
8680 Cambie Street
Vancouver, B.C. V6P 6M9

10 9

Chronicle Books
85 Second Street
San Francisco, CA 94105

Web Site: www.chronbooks.com

CONTENTS

ACKNOWLEDGMENTS

A Saturday afternoon in May, the backlot of 20th Century Fox Film Corp., a special invitation to see a new movie by George Lucas.... Something clicked. No, something *seismic* happened to me that day, for it was the start of a passion bordering on obsession that has occupied fully one-third of my life. Though there have been learned dissertations written about *Star Wars,* the real key to understanding it and its two sequels lies in one word: fun. That and the excitement of seeing unbounded energy and creativity pouring out of the screen. Let's not analyze it too deeply; let's just enjoy it. ★ That enjoyment, and a floor in my house filled with *Star Wars* merchandise and memorabilia, is what ultimately led to this book. But the shaping of the idea and the encouragement to proceed came from LucasArts Licensing's Lucy Wilson, one of George Lucas's longest and most loyal employees. She greased the wheels at Skywalker Ranch and provided full and complete access to the correspondence and photo archives that were so important to this book. ★ George Lucas was also generous with his time and recollections, despite a busy schedule. A tip of the hat, also, to his assistant, Jane Bay. ★ Thanks go to my new friends at Skywalker for their help. They include Kathleen Scanlon, Sue Rostoni, Julia Russo, Teresa Padilla, and Rachel Milstein in licensing and Don Bies, the story-filled prop archivist. I was also aided by photo librarians Halina Krukowski at Skywalker and Kerry Nordquist at Industrial Light & Magic. ★ The people at Kenner Products in Cincinnati were a huge help, but none more so than designer Mark Boudreaux. His infectious enthusiasm and days of work rummaging through his personal archives, finding and gathering material that was believed lost forever, and setting up a photo shoot were invaluable. We were both amazed to discover that his transcribed interview covered sixty pages—single spaced. Thanks also to Kenner's Jim Kipling for helping open the doors. ★ I was assisted by two excellent photographers, old friend Steve Essig in California and Kenner's David Tucker in Ohio. Other photography came from Kenner and Lucasfilm archives. Also assisting was Bobbie Cutler, who had the thankless job of transcribing some forty hours of taped interviews. And thanks to Randy Shilts for his gracious hospitality while I did my research in Northern California. ★ A special thanks to my colleagues in the Los Angeles news bureau of *The Wall Street Journal,* who had to cope with my somewhat erratic schedule, particularly my able assistant, Inga Loy, and my patient deputy, Roy Harris. ★ Lastly, my gratitude goes out to all the friends—both here and abroad—whom I've met in the last fifteen years, buying, selling, trading, or just talking about the world of Star Wars. I'll save a place for you in line in 1997!

A rare, early in-house premium: George Lucas ordered several hundred of these engraved Lucite stars to give out to members of the Lucasfilm team at a company premiere of Star Wars *in Marin County, California.*

LUKE SKYWALKER:

MASTER, MOVING STONES AROUND IS ONE THING. THIS (RAISING AN X-WING FIGHTER FROM A SWAMP) IS TOTALLY DIFFERENT.

YODA:

NO! NO DIFFERENT! ONLY DIFFERENT IN YOUR MIND. YOU MUST UNLEARN WHAT YOU HAVE LEARNED.

LUKE:

ALL RIGHT, I'LL GIVE IT A TRY.

YODA:

NO! TRY NOT. DO. OR DO NOT. THERE IS NO TRY.

— THE EMPIRE STRIKES BACK

CHAPTER 1

OUT OF
AGONY,
ECSTASY

George Lucas was in agony. Nothing about making this film was easy, but staring at the blank pile of blue lined paper in front of him— knowing that he had to make these script revisions, and soon—caused his mind to drift into the fantasy world he was trying to create. As tens of millions of people would find out just two years later, it was a strange world that Lucas was conjuring up: one that existed in a long-ago past, yet had all the trappings of the future; one that was far, far away, yet populated with

kindly aunts and properly gruff uncles as well as under-the-bed creatures and villains from a child's darkest nightmares.

⚡ Lucas took a sip of lukewarm coffee from his cup and mused, "Gee, wouldn't it be fun to have a Wookiee mug?" In 1975, a coffee mug sculpted in the likeness of an eight-foot-tall, two-hundred-year-old furry Wookiee named Chewbacca seemed about as far from reality as the possibility that *The Star Wars* and its two sequels would become three of the most popular motion pictures of all time. ⚡ Yet George Lucas, filmmaker, was about to become George Lucas, merchandiser par excellence, although that was about the furthest thing from his mind. For what Lucas was tweaking that day in the writing room of his Marin County, California, office was not only the script to a watershed film, but the beginning of a worldwide phenomenon. *The Star Wars*, soon to lose its initial

Chewbacca was, in some ways, patterned after George Lucas's dog, Indiana.

article but none of its fun and excitement, swept up audiences from Kansas City to Kuala Lumpur. While filmmaking is probably the most collaborative of arts, it took even more teamwork than usual to turn the denizens of the *Star Wars* universe into some of the most widely recognized cultural icons of the late twentieth century.

⚡ For the films themselves, Lucas gathered and challenged an unlikely team of industrial designers and engineers, welders, and oceanography majors to help him create a realistic-looking world that had existed only in his imagination. But where other filmmakers previously had succeeded in creating fantasy environments on screen, Lucas went beyond them to the real world. With the help of such people as an admitted "science fiction freak," a college senior, and a toy industry legend who went with his gut reaction even though he thought the film would fade away in two months,

the world of *Star Wars* got translated into such things as toys, T-shirts, bubble bath lotion, and even marshmallow candies that fed a near-insatiable worldwide demand to own a tangible piece of the fantasy. ⚡ While *Star Wars* toys didn't start filling the shelves until early 1978, the cry for them was so great during the 1977 Christmas season that Kenner Products decided to sell what

even its then president concedes were basically "empty boxes" with a promise to deliver some small action figures within a few months. It worked. Thousands of Early Bird Certificate Kits were sold for up to $16 each. Today, collectors pay $200 or more for a sealed kit and the follow-up package of four action figures. ⚡ The films' major characters became instantly recognizable.

The 20th Century Fox distributor in Berlin did a version of this poster with each film's logo. It features headlines about the Reagan Administration's Strategic Defense Initiative, which had been dubbed Star Wars. *It urges that* Star Wars *be kept only on the cinema screen.*

Editorial cartoonists found in the menacing Darth Vader an ideal new way to portray the Soviet Union as an "Evil Empire," and later Yoda as the font of all wisdom and ethics. Parodies of the fussy golden robot, C-3PO, and his stalwart companion, R2-D2, found their way into everything from *Mad* magazine to X-rated takeoffs. And although Lucas still hates the comparison, President Ronald Reagan's grandiose and futuristic Strategic Defense Initiative was dubbed the *Star Wars* defense by critics and the media, certainly helping the language of the films become part of everyday life.

⚡ The impact of *Star Wars* can be measured in many ways. On strictly a bottom-line basis, the three films themselves collected a total of about $1.3 billion worldwide at the box office and millions more through video sales and rentals. Merchandise sales have added up to more than $2.5 billion. In today's dollars, the films' footprints might translate into as much as $6 billion to $7 billion. To boot, *Star Wars* jump-started the slow-growing licensing business and was responsible for the now-taken-for-granted licensing of major movies for products ranging from novels and trading cards to toys and clothing. In fact, according to the trade publication, *The Licensing Letter,* prior to the release of *Star Wars* in May 1977, consumers worldwide spent less than $5 billion a year for licensed merchandise. By 1990 that figure had topped $66 billion.

⚡ As for filmmaking itself, *Star Wars* ushered in a new era in films—entertainment filled with glorious special effects and strong story lines. When the giant Star Destroyer thundered over the heads of audiences after *Star Wars'* now-famous opening crawl, Lucas not only grabbed the youngsters at whom he was aiming his myth, but also awoke childhood memories in countless adults.

⚡ Aside from introducing the most astounding and realistic

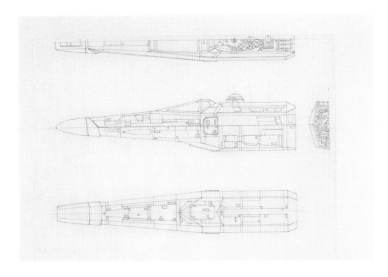

This is where it all began:
Jack Farrah's pattern based on
Jim Swearingen's drawing layout
for Kenner's first Star Wars
vehicle, the X-Wing Fighter.

➤ **STAR WARS FACTOID** ◄

In March 1978, Beverly Hills, California, patent attorney Peter Eicher sent 20th Century Fox Film Corp. a *''VERY URGENT''* letter. He informed studio lawyers that the federal government had suspended a request for a foreign design patent on Luke Skywalker's X-Wing Fighter ''until a review requested by both NASA and the Air Force,...on the basis that the application contains subject matter that appears to be of interest to the National Security....'' The KGB, it seems, would have been better off spending a Saturday at the flicks than trying to snoop around U.S. defense plants.

alien characters, props, and vehicles, *Star Wars* ushered in a new era of visual effects. New ways of filming with computer-controlled cameras were devised, and special printing techniques for the film —allowing two dozen or more different elements to be added to one frame—were pushed to the limits. As well, *Star Wars* was one of the first feature films to make important use of then-emerging computer graphics techniques. ⚡ The *Star Wars* phenomenon had its Dark Side too. The film spawned mindless imitations in which loud and off-kilter special effects were the stars, and good writing and plot were ignored. It also led to a glut of teenage exploitation films that attempted—usually unsuccessfully—to strive for the new blockbuster status of selling $100 million of tickets at the box office. ⚡ How did it all come together? How did *Star Wars* go from an idea in the mind of a young filmmaker to beautifully rendered paintings, then to props so realistic that the government delayed granting one a design patent on the grounds of "national security," and finally to toys with such jaw-breaking names as "Darth Vader's Star Destroyer Action Playset"? Rarely in the recent annals of popular culture has there been such a fortuitous interaction between thinkers and doers, artists and builders, and marketers and merchandisers. ⚡ Creativity, easy to admire, is hard to fully explain. The timing certainly was right in the arenas of both film and merchandising. Lucas, who originally wanted to do a new Flash Gordon film with the spirit of the Saturday matinee serials he saw as a child in Modesto, California, was a master synthesizer with the mythic vision to get the ball rolling. But to pull it all off, to make the kind of mark it did, *Star Wars* had to have something else going for it. Was it just plain dumb luck? Or was it...the Force?

REMEMBER, A JEDI CAN FEEL THE FORCE FLOWING THROUGH HIM.

YOU MEAN IT CONTROLS YOUR ACTIONS?

PARTIALLY. BUT IT ALSO OBEYS YOUR COMMANDS.

— STAR WARS

D O

H A M B U R G E R S

R E A L L Y

F L Y ?

The huge commercial success of Lucas's second film, *American Graffiti*, made it possible for him to tackle his space fantasy project. Yet the going was never easy. Two studios passed on it before Alan Ladd, Jr., head of production at 20th Century Fox, took a gamble on *Star Wars*. Lucas surrounded himself with creative types he had met while attending the University of Southern California film school, or with people they knew. In doing so, he helped give birth to a new era in the art of movie special effects

with the creation of Industrial Light & Magic (ILM), a group of film magicians who are still advancing the frontiers of movie making. The soft-spoken Lucas rarely made waves or showed much outward emotion in the presence of these collaborators. For while he clearly was conductor of the assembled band, he let the artists and craftsmen he selected have a major role in orchestrating the composition. ⚡ Two of the most important contributors to *Star Wars'* look and texture were production illustrator Ralph McQuarrie, who had been a technical illustrator for Boeing, and effects illustrator and designer Joe Johnston, who later became a film director himself. Also included on the team were artist Nilo Rodis-Jamero; special effects wizards Richard Edlund, Dennis Muren, and John Dykstra; model builders Lorne Peterson, Steve Gawley, and Mike Fulmer; stop-motion animators Phil Tippett and Jon Berg; production designers John Barry and Norman Reynolds; costume designer John Mollo; and creature masters Stuart Freeborn and Rick Baker. ⚡ Today, the look of the *Star Wars* universe is taken for granted, and the films made the design work look almost effortless. It wasn't. "Designing that universe was very complicated and time-consuming," Lucas notes. "We couldn't go out to the store and buy things; we had to design everything from the forks and plates to the clothing and binoculars, to all the transportation vehicles and spaceships. You have to figure out communications devices, computers, even wall panels in a hallway. And everything has to look like it fits." ⚡ Of course, some reference to the *existing* universe is not only unavoidable but helpful in giving visual cues to both creator and audience. Lucas himself suggested that the Rebel Cruiser, aboard which Luke is fitted with a new hand at the end of *The Empire Strikes Back*, be based on the shape

LEFT:
The basic shape of Slave I, bounty hunter Boba Fett's craft, was derived from the unusual shape of some street lamps near the headquarters of Industrial Light & Magic.

RIGHT:
*Lucasfilm's initial model maker,
Colin Cantwell, built this
preliminary Star Destroyer.*

INSET:
*Some early concept doodles for
the Star Destroyer.*

OPPOSITE PAGE:
*The Rebel Cruiser is based on
the shape of an outboard motor
at George Lucas's suggestion.
It was designed by Joe Johnston
and Nilo Rodis-Jamero.*

➤ STAR WARS FACTOID ◄

What's in a name? If it's Darth Vader's massive Star Destroyer spaceship and it's named Executor, plenty. Kenner asked that it be allowed to call the ship something else due to the "aura" the name Executor might have as presented in a television commercial or on a package directed at kids. So Kenner challenged its ad agency, Grey Advertising, to come up with an alternative. The ad folks came up with a list of 153 possibilities, ranging from the cartoonish (Starbase Malevolent) to the demonic (Black Coven) to the mythologic (Haphaestus VII) to the just plain silly (Cosmocurse). However, the list didn't include the simplest and now-obvious final choice: Darth Vader's Star Destroyer.

of an outboard motor. Johnston and Rodis-Jamero added such incredibly complex detailing to the basic shape (the ILM model makers bashed plastic model kits and used miniature boat hulls, a B-29 fuselage, and small-scale aircraft carriers to build it) that the cruiser is one of the few vehicles that was never turned into either a toy or commercial model kit. Lorne Peterson, supervising model maker at ILM, is convinced that the distinctive domed towers on the bridge of the massive Star Destroyer were at least subconsciously inspired by a view from Lucas's house of similar towers at a deactivated Nike missile base. The shape of Boba Fett's Slave I ship was inspired by unusual hooded street lamps near ILM headquarters. ⚡ "Sometimes I wrote very minimal descriptions of certain vehicles and characters," Lucas recalls. "So I'd sit down with one of the design artists or a group of them and tell how I'd

For close-up scenes in the "Tatooine desert," just the bottom part of the massive Jawa Sandcrawler was built.

written about a character or vehicle in the script, and then talk about it in much more detail. Then they'd go off and draw concepts." ⚡ McQuarrie, for example, came up with the original concept for the Sandcrawler, the huge transport used by the Jawas —the hooded creatures with glowing orange eyes who travel the trackless wastelands of Tatooine collecting and selling scrap. But McQuarrie's meticulous preproduction painting was almost *too* beautiful for a Jawa vehicle. So Johnston and the model makers gave the Sandcrawler additional sharp angles and pushed its proportions more out of whack. ⚡ Lucas would often use a handy rubber stamp to give his reaction to the drawings. "WONDERFUL!" one read. "OK" and "NOT SO GREAT" meant try again. When *The Empire Strikes Back* and *Return of the Jedi* rolled around, a more flush Lucas had an additional option: Creature by Committee. "I'd assign a character to maybe five different guys and each might come up with ten different designs," Lucas says. "I'd tell them I like this part of this one, that part of that one and so on, and whoever came the closest would take the other elements and start refining the design." ⚡ Even when Lucas had a clear idea of what he wanted, such as the menacing look of Darth Vader, he was open to suggestions for an even better design. "Vader was mentioned in the script as some sort of dark lord of the evil side," McQuarrie remembers. "With the desert setting so prominent, I think George at first envisioned him as a Bedouin-like character. He suggested that maybe Vader could be in a silk robe that always fluttered as he came in, and he might have his face covered with black silk and have some kind of big helmet like a Japanese warrior. ⚡ "I reminded George that the first time we see Vader, he's boarding one spaceship from another and I asked, 'How's he

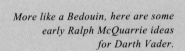
More like a Bedouin, here are some early Ralph McQuarrie ideas for Darth Vader.

going to breathe out there in space?' So my illustrations show a breathing mask with a downward-curving snout and big goggles. John Barry and his designers developed it further with a mask that gave Vader a tremendously monumental stature, and I think George felt that keeping Vader always in his mask would be fascinating—like an actor in an old Greek tragedy. But it all came to pass because I thought he needed a mask to breathe." ⚡ Some of the earliest spacecraft models came from model builder Colin Cantwell, but they were mostly too streamlined for Lucas, who wanted the look of a grittier universe, where people actually lived and worked and occasionally dinged their dirty landspeeders. So a key ship, Han Solo's Millennium Falcon, evolved from a long and sleek craft that looked vaguely like something from the TV series *Space: 1999* to a ship that looks a bit like Lucas's favorite food. It was even dubbed the Flying Hamburger. ⚡ In fact, when Lucas ordered just that—a plain hamburger—at a five-star French restaurant in Cincinnati on his first visit to Kenner, he told the toy makers that burgers were quite important—and were the inspiration for the Falcon's design. As for the ship's cockpit, Lucas told his hosts, just imagine an olive off to one side. Food allusions abounded at ILM. A twin-fuselage Imperial TIE Fighter was called a "double chili TIE" because it reminded some folks of two chili dogs. ⚡ With limited money and even less time, very little went to waste on *Star Wars*. The first prop model of the original Millennium Falcon was stripped of its paint, modified a bit, and then covered with little parts from bashed commercial model kits—a favorite technique of ILM model builders—to give it more detail. It then became the Rebel Blockade Runner, the ship on which Princess Leia makes her

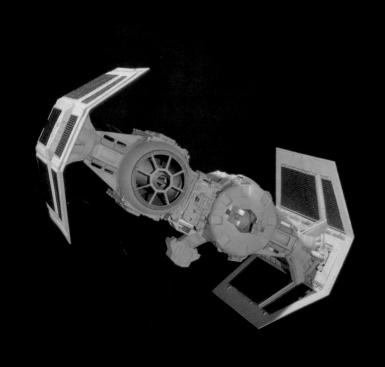

unsuccessful attempt to escape the clutches of Darth Vader. ⚡ What wasn't used in *Star Wars* also had a way of cropping up later in the trilogy—even whole environments. The Bespin Cloud City in *The Empire Strikes Back*, for example, was in an early draft of *Star Wars* as an Imperial prison fortress. ⚡ One of the earliest ships designed was the T-16 Skyhopper, Luke's suborbital hot rod, which he used to joyride around Tatooine, chasing womp rats and splitting canyons with just barely inches to spare. Colin Cantwell built a simple model of the small three-winged craft, and Luke plays with the model itself in his garage near the beginning of *Star Wars*. There just wasn't enough time or money to shoot an intended scene using the Skyhopper, so a detailed prop was never built. But the classic design was too good to waste, and a much larger and more detailed version came back in *Return of the Jedi*

OPPOSITE PAGE,TOP:

Han Solo's Millennium Falcon, seen bottom up, is the key ship in the Trilogy. Does it remind you of a popular fast food?

OPPOSITE PAGE, BOTTOM:

The model makers at Industrial Light & Magic always seemed to be hungry. They nicknamed this the Double Chili TIE Fighter after a couple of chili dogs.

BELOW:

This vehicle was supposed to be the Millennium Falcon, but Lucas decided to go in a different direction. With modifications, this Colin Cantwell model became the basis for the Rebel Blockade Runner.

INSET, LEFT:

One of the few major vehicles never made into a toy was the Rebel Blockade Runner, here in a preliminary design drawing that shows proposed scale changes.

INSET, RIGHT:

ILM's Rebel Blockade Runner gets ready to whiz by in the opening scene of Star Wars.

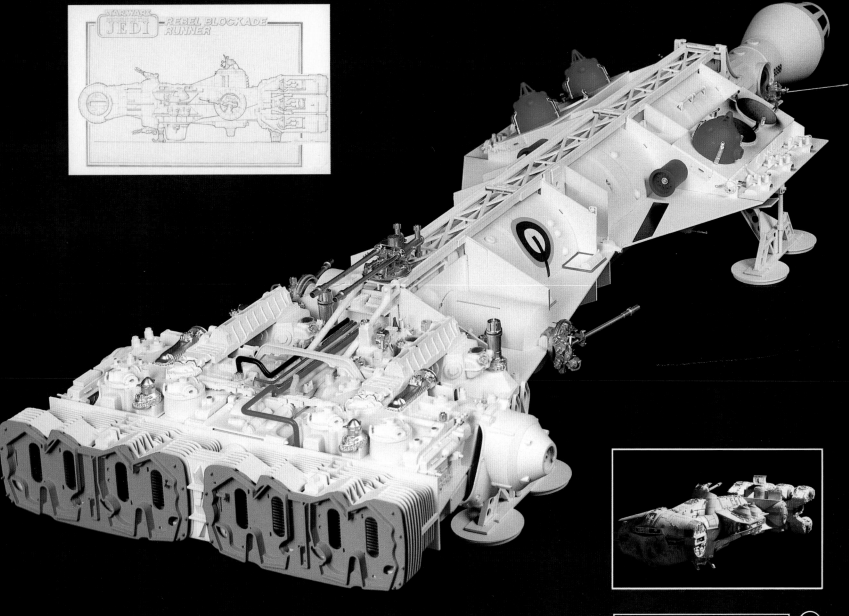

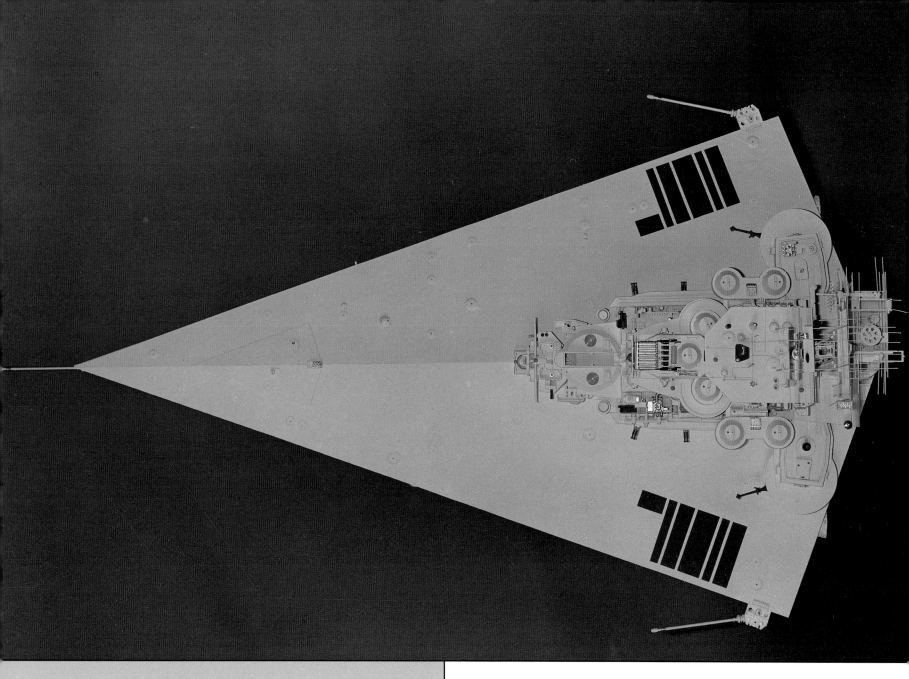

ABOVE:
Overhead view of Colin Cantwell's initial model for the Star Destroyer.

RIGHT:
Earliest model of the TIE Fighter by Cantwell.

as the Imperial Shuttle—actually three different shuttles, although only one large-sized model was built. There were several design variations for the Shuttle, as Johnston, Rodis-Jamero, Reynolds, and McQuarrie all contributed sketches. Finally, Johnston dashed off a quick sketch of a TIE Fighter fuselage with the three wings of the Skyhopper, further modified the cabin, and the Shuttle—one of the more elegant-looking ships of the *Star Wars* universe—was born. ⚡ But a final design wasn't necessarily a *final* design. Building a costume that an actor could wear and move around in sometimes required further changes in the workshop or even on the set in order to make it function in the real world. And as the vehicle sketches were turned into models, ILM's visual specialists would also order changes: thicken a TIE Fighter wing support to prevent vibration as it's suspended from a rod to be filmed; add bulk to a Star Destroyer antenna to make sure it photographs well; and turn a "bubble" canopy over the X-Wing cockpit into a seven-section segmented canopy to do away with reflections when it's lighted and filmed. ⚡ Often when a director or other major luminary on a film asks, "So what do you think?" the question is purely rhetorical. *Star Wars* was clearly a film on which an answer was not only expected, but often followed.

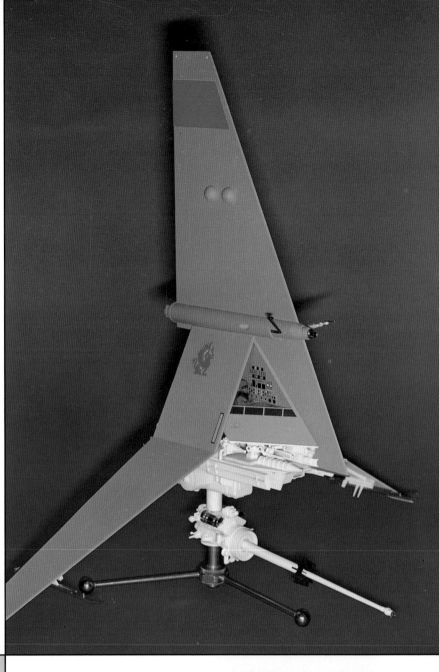

ABOVE:
Cantwell's model for Luke Skywalker's Skyhopper vehicle. In the movie, Luke actually played with the model in his garage. The full-scale version wasn't built, but the design later evolved into the Imperial Shuttle.

RIGHT:
One of the most elegant-looking spacecraft, the Imperial Shuttle evolved from the Skyhopper. One main model served as three different shuttles in Return of the Jedi.

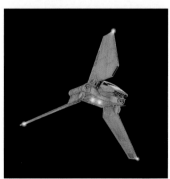

YODA:

I am wondering, why are you here?

LUKE SKYWALKER:

I'm looking for someone.

LOOKING? FOUND SOME-ONE, YOU HAVE, I WOULD SAY, HMMM?

—THE EMPIRE STRIKES BACK

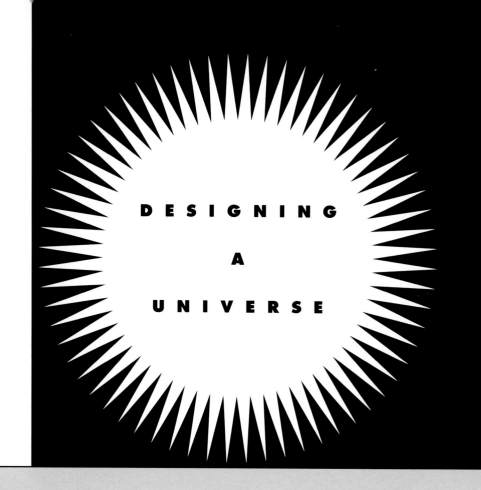

It was pure coincidence. Illustrator Ralph McQuarrie was working at Encyclopedia Britannica Films in Los Angeles in 1967 when a student film-maker came over to screen his latest project, a chilling look at a sterile future world called *THX 1138:4EB*. However, it wasn't until four years later, as *THX 1138* was being turned into a feature-length film, that McQuarrie actually met George Lucas. A onetime technical artist at Boeing, McQuarrie had done some paintings for two of Lucas's writer friends who were trying to

get financing for a science fiction movie. McQuarrie was living in a small garage apartment when Lucas and a few associates visited to chat and look through slides of his science fiction art. ⚡ "George talked about *Star Wars*, although it didn't have a title then," McQuarrie says. "But he spoke about this sprawling, galactic war picture and I told him: 'It sounds great. I'd love to see it.'" Neither man knew it at the time, but Lucas had found his Boswell of the brush, the man who would come up with the visual images to match Lucas's words. A few years went by, and after United Artists and Universal Studios had passed on the thirteen-page treatment for *The Star Wars*, Lucas and producer Gary Kurtz paid McQuarrie another visit. ⚡ "From the treatment, the movie came across as vastly ambitious, but a bit hokey, and those studios just didn't understand it," McQuarrie says. "I think George and Gary called me in because they were worried they were going to run out of studios. This film was going to be one gigantic moving science fiction illustration, so they wanted to have something visual to show Fox." ⚡ Actually, Fox's Alan Ladd had signed a deal memo with Lucas two years before, based on a screening of *American Graffiti* and a detailed discussion about the space epic. But a nervous and somewhat perplexed Fox board of directors still had to approve funding this strange film, and Lucas and Kurtz wanted to be well prepared. McQuarrie was hired in the summer of 1975 on a week-to-week basis, and in less than three weeks had come up with scores of rough sketches that he turned into five sweeping panoramas capturing the feel of the film. The art was a key to getting *Star Wars* past its final hurdle. ⚡ "This was the first time I had worked on something that wasn't meant for publication, and every little detail wasn't going to be scrutinized, so I felt very

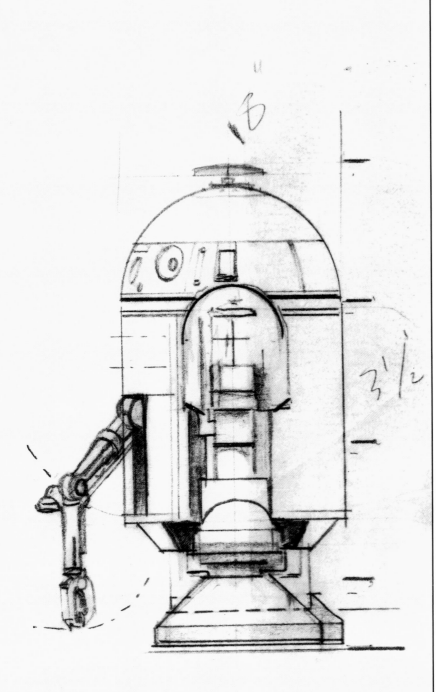

relaxed about it," McQuarrie remembers. Unlike many preproduction sketches, these were finished paintings and they helped Fox officials visualize Lucas's dream; the artwork also gave them confidence that a film populated with weird characters in bizarre settings actually could be made. ⚡ McQuarrie's initial acrylic and gouache paintings included a scene of the robots C-3PO and R2-D2 trekking across the Tatooine desert; the giant Jawa Sandcrawler; and the lightsaber battle between Darth Vader and Obi Wan Kenobi. The three-week job turned into near full-time employment through the release of *Jedi* in 1983, with McQuarrie also doing some of the special background matte paintings that were seen in the films. ⚡ Later there would be criticism that some of the visuals in *Star Wars* were borrowed, that a certain ship looked as if it could have come from a Flash Gordon serial, or that a character might have been based on one from *John Carter of Mars*. But that was part of Lucas's genius: to create a wondrous pastiche from the best of science fantasy and mythology and wrap it in his own special package. "What George did," McQuarrie says, "was expand the vision and scope of the earlier films and make everything more believable." ⚡ When McQuarrie sits down to draw, he tries to clear his mind. He starts with one line, then lets his pencil, and his subconscious, take him someplace he hadn't thought of when he started. Originally his subconscious led him astray about Han Solo. "In my mind, he was a much more dapper sort of fellow. In fact, I saw him looking a bit like George—beard and all—but dressed up in really tailored clothes. George was correct in assessing the effect of the elaborate costume; it sort of takes over. George wanted the *character* to be important, not have a costumed doll on screen." ⚡ Production designer John

*Ralph McQuarrie's early concept
sketches for Yoda.*

A *Johnston* 0152
2/78

*Early design drawing
for Chewbacca.*

*Yoda, or a miniature Santa Claus?
This illustration is part of the
creative process that resulted in the
final appearance of the Jedi Master.*

*The look of the Ewoks was tough
to pin down. In this illustration,
Ralph McQuarrie is getting close.*

Barry and costume designer John Mollo, both of whom won Academy Awards for *Star Wars* (the film was awarded a total of seven), were free to use as much or as little of McQuarrie's work as they saw fit, so there were further changes. But much of the rich detail and the overall feel of the artist's work, and that of Joe Johnston, came through in the film. ⚡ McQuarrie and Johnston had little time to admire their work. Just months after the huge opening of *Star Wars*, they were hard at work on the sequel. Lucas hadn't gotten very far into the script, but he had some ideas and he shared them with the two men. "He started talking about a battle in the snow," McQuarrie recalls. "And he talked about either some sort of castle in the snow or Darth Vader's castle in a far-off mountain retreat—and that fascinated me, although it never made it to the final script. We had regular meetings at which Joe and I would lay out our sketches, and maybe Joe would have a great idea to embellish one of mine and vice versa." ⚡ McQuarrie says that he tends toward an elegant and clean, streamlined look in his art. Since Lucas was looking for more of a lived-in look, he had to restrain himself. But the moderne style was perfectly acceptable for the futuristic Bespin Cloud City, which had curves everywhere a straight line would normally be. ⚡ Johnston has gone on to become a film director, but that wasn't a course McQuarrie pursued—though he was tempted. "I was so enthusiastic," McQuarrie says. "George would come by and I'd start talking to him about all my directing ideas and he'd tell me—very gently—not to worry about that stuff, but to get on with my design work. He was right of course, but I tend to get carried away. That's part of what makes me an artist and why I always want things to be as good as they can be."

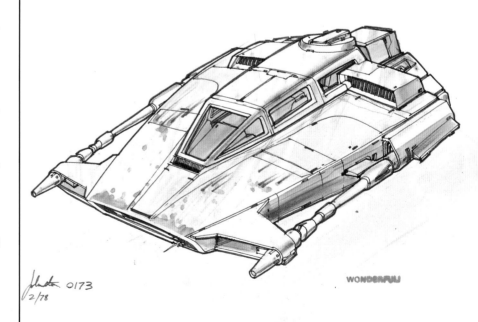

RIGHT:
A preliminary sketch by Joe Johnston for the all-important X-Wing Fighter.

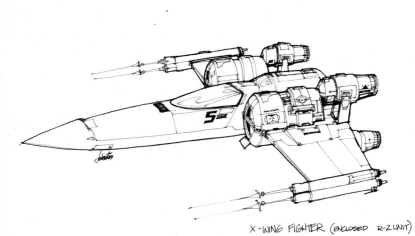

X-WING FIGHTER (ENCLOSED R-2 UNIT)

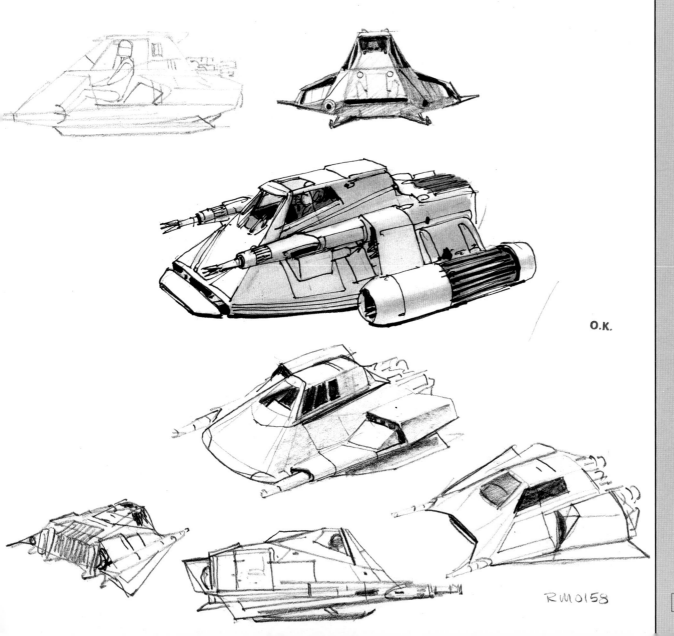

O.K.

RM 0158

OPPOSITE PAGE AND LEFT:
Dozens of detailed illustrations such as these by Joe Johnson and Ralph McQuarrie were done before the final look of the Snowspeeder was chosen.

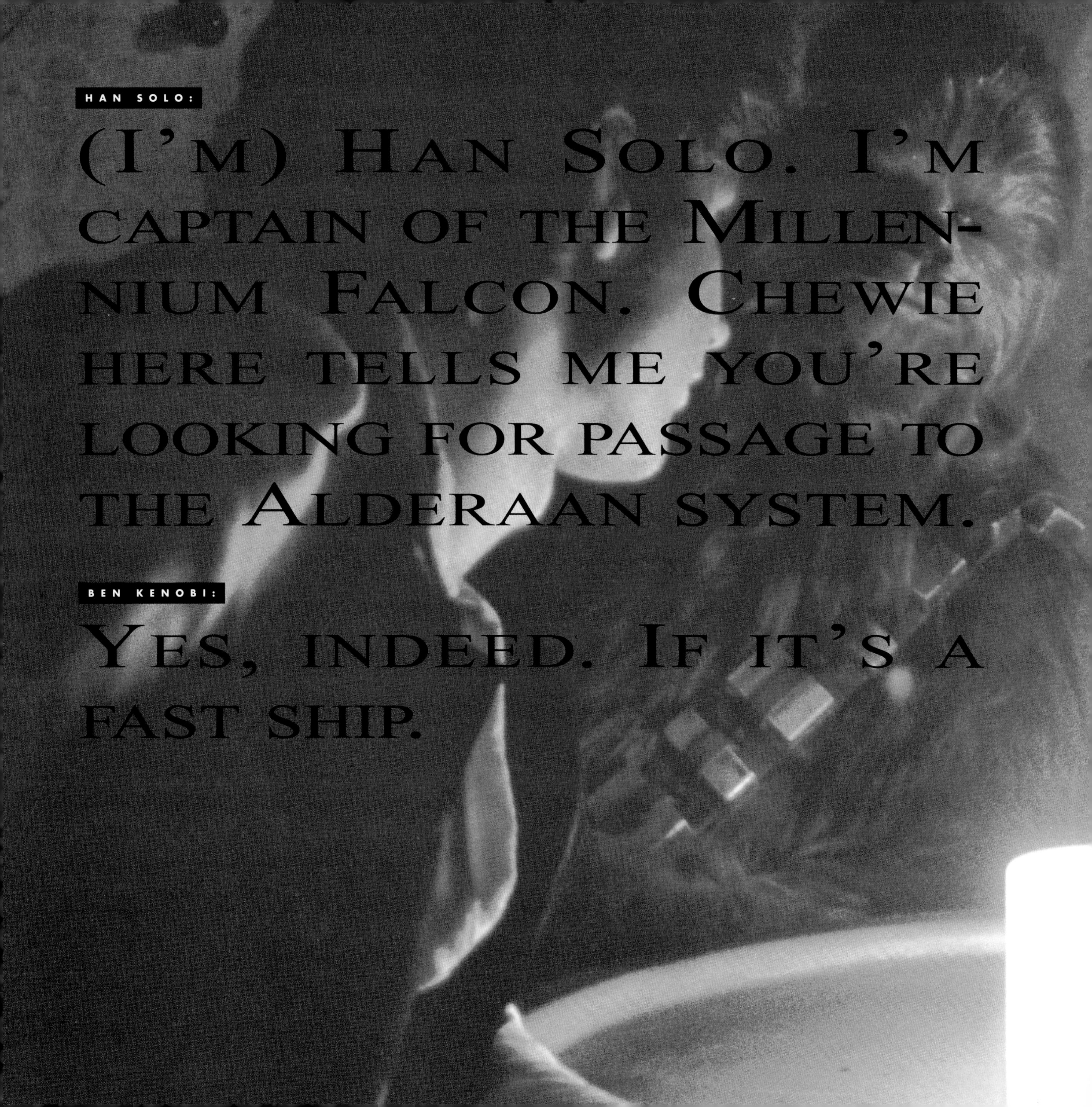

HAN SOLO:

(I'm) Han Solo. I'm captain of the Millennium Falcon. Chewie here tells me you're looking for passage to the Alderaan system.

BEN KENOBI:

Yes, indeed. If it's a fast ship.

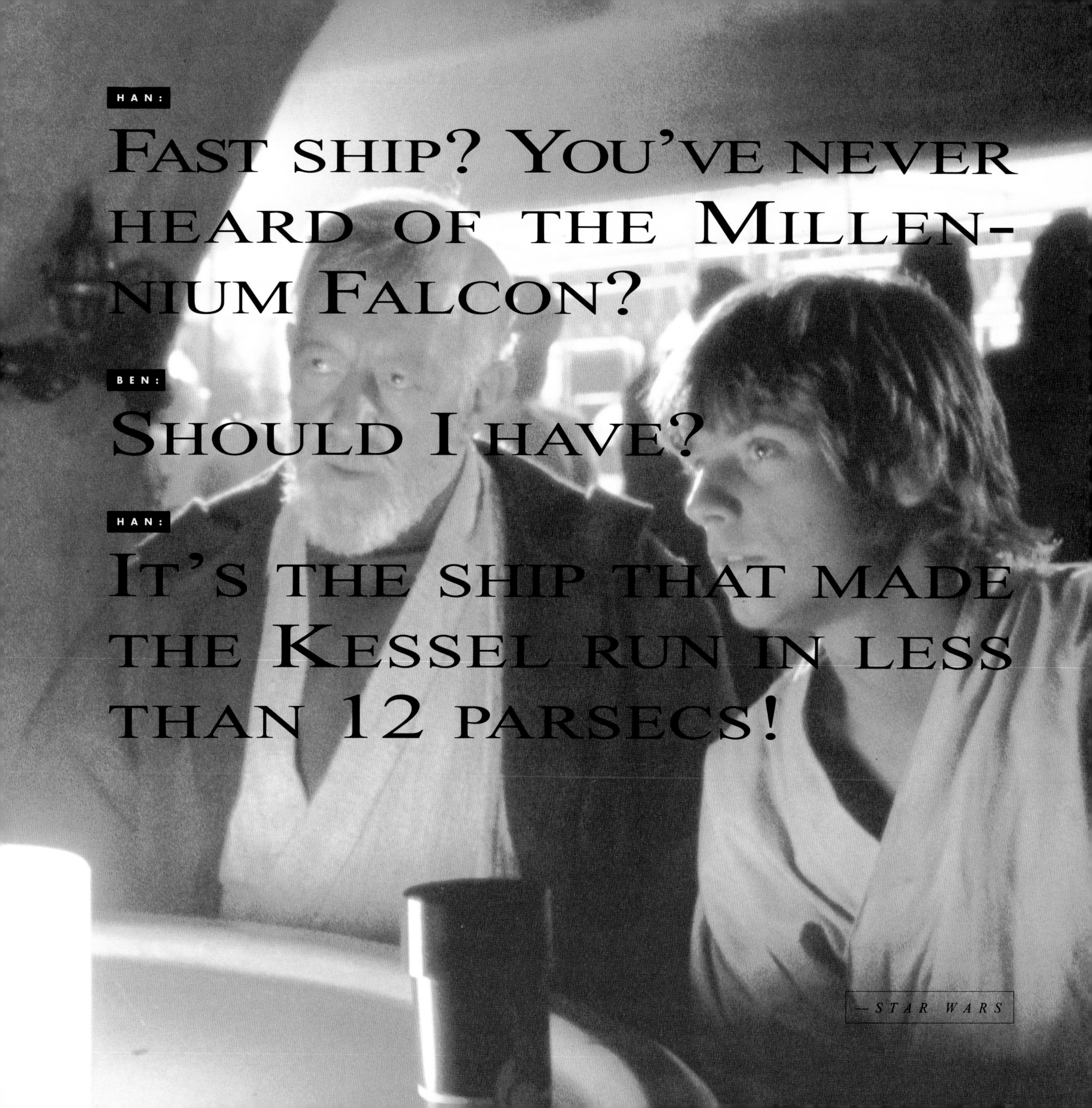

HAN:

FAST SHIP? YOU'VE NEVER HEARD OF THE MILLENNIUM FALCON?

BEN:

SHOULD I HAVE?

HAN:

IT'S THE SHIP THAT MADE THE KESSEL RUN IN LESS THAN 12 PARSECS!

—STAR WARS

BUILDING

THE

DREAM

Visualizing a spaceship that looks like a flying hamburger with an olive

for a cockpit is a big enough leap. Building it and the scores of other

vehicles, creatures, and sets that filled the *Star Wars* universe seemed like an

impossibility, especially given the time and budgetary constraints.

Visual effects ace Dennis Muren and a band of about seventy others—mostly

young and inexperienced in the ways of Hollywood—toughed it out and

overcame roadblocks with creative solutions that became the basis of the

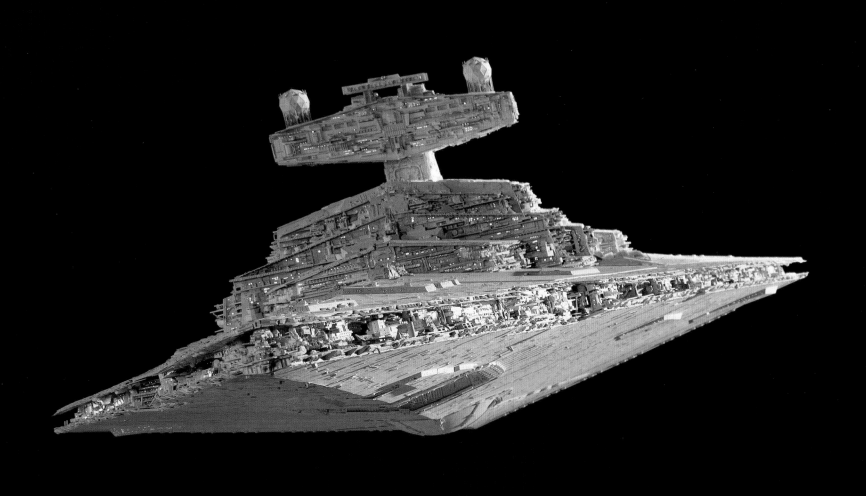

*The final version of the Star
Destroyer, built in several different
sizes, was meant in filmic terms
to be about six miles long.*

ABOVE:
*Imperial All Terrain Armored
Transports, built by ILM's
Phil Tippett and Jon Berg, attack
a Rebel base on Hoth.*

OPPOSITE PAGE:
*A Joe Johnston development
sketch of an AT-AT.*

there was no script! And George would say, 'Don't worry about that; just do storyboards!' The process then was to lay out random shots and pick out some that would conceivably work. George would work on the script at home while I would be working on the boards. During our meetings, he would pick out shots that he felt looked promising and write them in. It was a very unusual evolution." The sequence kept changing even after filming began. ⚡ Within bounds, the model makers were given lots of freedom. "Sometimes something that's drawn just can't be built, because planes just don't intersect like lines do," Peterson says. "So we had a lot of leeway. And Joe Johnston and the others didn't usually draw every single detail. I remember in *Star Wars* working a lot on the back section of the Millennium Falcon and doing kind of a mandala composition that worked out real well. Boy, the back of that ship was detailed with parts from plastic kits of motorcycles, panzer tanks, eighteen-wheel truck tires, and rims and engine cases off Formula One racing cars." ⚡ What makes a good model maker? Mike Fulmer, who was an oil field welder and part-time model maker before he joined ILM for *The Empire Strikes Back*, puts it this way: "You have to be an engineer, painter, machinist, metal worker, mold maker, pattern maker, chemist—and half nuts. You work ten to twelve hours a day detailing an area that's no bigger than a saucer." ⚡ Detailing of the models involved not only bashing commercial hobby kits, but using everyday household objects such as medicine bottle caps. Lines would be etched onto the surface of models to simulate panels and other possible openings. And because the world of *Star Wars* was a "used" one, the prop makers didn't have the usual worry of fingerprint smudges messing up a pristine paint job; in fact, they probably added

something. ⚡ Phil Tippett and Jon Berg were hired on *Star Wars* toward the end of production when a hurry-up call went out to shoot new footage to beef up the now-famous Cantina sequence that had been shot in England. Lucas hired effects makeup and mask artist Rick Baker who, because time was short, used a number of creature getups he had already made as well as some new ones the crew cobbled together. ⚡ "We all played creatures," Tippett says. "People from ILM, secretaries, model makers—everybody had something dripping out of a huge nose or stuff coming out of strange eyes, and we all said it was the most fun we ever had on a picture!" ⚡ Lucas was also casting around for new ideas for the "holographic" chess game sequence in the film. He had planned to have actors in creature costumes move around on a large-scale chess board, then double-expose the film to simulate a hologram, but *Westworld* had done something similar and he wanted a different look. Tippett and Berg had been working in Rick Baker's creature shop on stop-motion animation puppets—where near-imperceptible moves are made to jointed models as film is exposed frame by frame, leading to motion when the film is projected at regular speed. They already had made jointed papier-mâché puppets for a personal project they were pursuing, and the chess sequence became the last one shot for *Star Wars*. ⚡ Tippett and Berg's role expanded greatly in *The Empire Strikes Back*. They helped construct and animate the Tauntaun, the large horned snow creature used as Rebel transportation on Hoth, and the mighty Imperial AT-ATs, the near-invincible walking tanks officially dubbed All Terrain Armored Transports. Some of the filmmakers thought the Tauntaun would work better as a man in a suit, and others insisted that a full-sized motorized Tauntaun be built

➤ STAR WARS FACTOID ◄

A tasty promotion: A few weeks after *Star Wars*
opened, The Broadway department store chain in
Southern California offered in its tearooms *"The
Force Be With You"* Luncheon. The menu
included "succulent juices from Luke Skywalker's
moisture farm, a delicious fourth moon of Yavin
sandwich of Swiss cheese, tomato and fresh alfalfa
sprouts, plus a spice cookie [in the shape] of R2-
D2 or the star ship. Try it...It's out of this
world!" Only $2.85, but that didn't include admis-
sion to the Cantina for a drink afterwards.

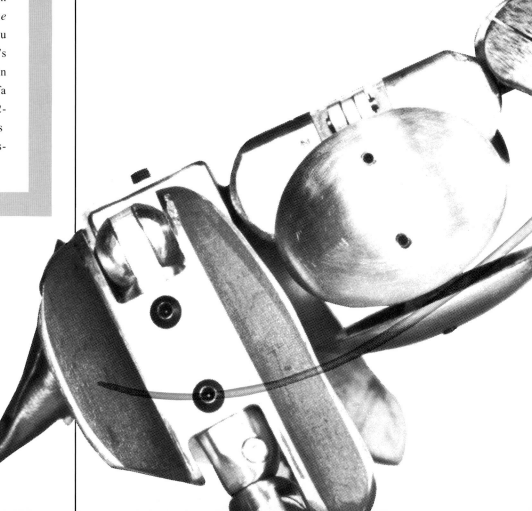

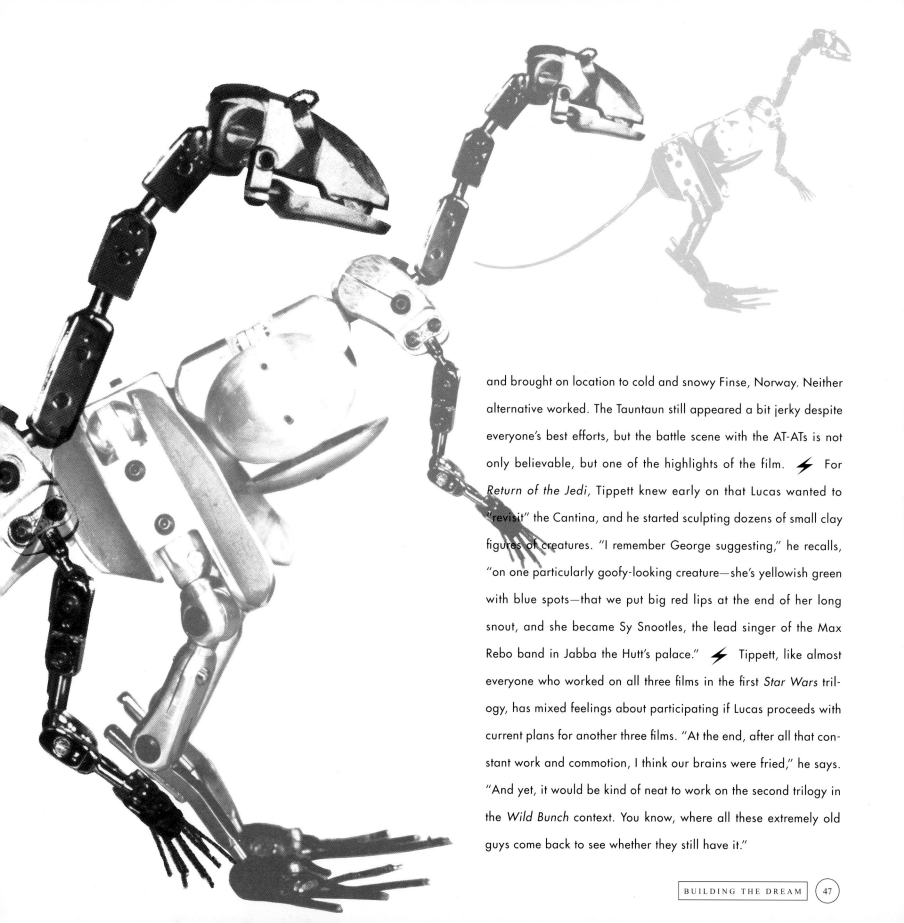

and brought on location to cold and snowy Finse, Norway. Neither alternative worked. The Tauntaun still appeared a bit jerky despite everyone's best efforts, but the battle scene with the AT-ATs is not only believable, but one of the highlights of the film. ⚡ For *Return of the Jedi*, Tippett knew early on that Lucas wanted to "revisit" the Cantina, and he started sculpting dozens of small clay figures of creatures. "I remember George suggesting," he recalls, "on one particularly goofy-looking creature—she's yellowish green with blue spots—that we put big red lips at the end of her long snout, and she became Sy Snootles, the lead singer of the Max Rebo band in Jabba the Hutt's palace." ⚡ Tippett, like almost everyone who worked on all three films in the first *Star Wars* trilogy, has mixed feelings about participating if Lucas proceeds with current plans for another three films. "At the end, after all that constant work and commotion, I think our brains were fried," he says. "And yet, it would be kind of neat to work on the second trilogy in the *Wild Bunch* context. You know, where all these extremely old guys come back to see whether they still have it."

HAN SOLO:

I'M NOT GOING ANYWHERE...

LUKE SKYWALKER:

BUT THEY'RE GOING TO KILL HER!

HAN:

BETTER HER THAN ME...

LUKE:

SHE'S RICH.

HAN:

RICH?

YES. RICH, POWERFUL!
LISTEN, IF YOU WERE TO
RESCUE HER, THE REWARD
WOULD BE...MORE WEALTH
THAN YOU CAN IMAGINE.

I DON'T KNOW, I CAN
IMAGINE QUITE A BIT!

OF DOGS AND MUGS AND WOOKIEES

Nobody expected to get *really* rich, least of all George Lucas. After the success of *American Graffiti*, he could have renegotiated his Fox contract to get more than triple the $150,000 the studio had agreed to pay him to write and direct *Star Wars*. But for Lucas, control was more important than cash, and one of the things he insisted having control over— or at least joint control with Fox—was any merchandising of his film. Not that Lucas expected a retail bonanza. A decade before, Fox had

released *Doctor Dolittle* with a large merchandising push. Both the film and the products bombed, and toy and novelty manufacturers were still treating movie tie-ins like the plague. "Merchandising was mainly to help promote a film," Lucas notes, "and manufacturers were much more interested in tying in to television programming, because that gave them a much longer time frame in which to operate." ⚡ Lucas says he got involved in merchandising—something he concedes he knew little about—primarily to protect the film. "I didn't want manufacturers slapping the *Star Wars* name on everything under the sun and cheapening it. It was definitely a control issue. I wanted quality as well as a promotional kick, and I just felt my own team could be more sensitive to all the issues than any studio with a lot of other films to worry about." ⚡ The young director really didn't have toys or coffee mugs on the brain when he was populating his fantasy world. "When you're sitting and writing all day long you ruminate," Lucas says. "It wasn't, 'Gee, I could turn Chewie into a Wookiee mug and R2-D2 into a cookie jar and make a lot of money.' It was simply that the design of R2 reminded me of a cookie jar, and I thought it would be funny to lift his top off and grab a cookie. As for Chewbacca, since my dog was sort of a prototype for him, and they sell these mugs of your favorite breed of dog, it occurred to me that it might be fun to have a Chewbacca mug sitting on my writing desk." And, in fact, the Chewbacca mug, beautifully sculpted by ceramic artist Jim Rumpf, and the R2-D2 pottery cookie jar are among Lucas's favorite pieces of merchandise from the trilogy. ⚡ While Lucas and producer Gary Kurtz were somewhat involved in the early merchandising efforts, they largely left the grunt work to Charles Lippincott, then one of only a handful of full-time Lucasfilm

employees, who originally was hired to generate publicity for *Star Wars*. Lippincott had gone to the University of Southern California film school with Lucas and remembers sitting on the curb outside a computer lab talking with him for hours about his student film, *THX 1138*. Lippincott had become a film publicist at MGM and bumped into Kurtz in August 1975; the producer told him about a science fantasy film that Lucas was writing and directing. ⚡ Lippincott joined Lucasfilm three months later with a title so long he almost needed two business cards to fit it in: vice-president for advertising, publicity, promotion, and merchandising. Within a few weeks, the first merchandising deal had been struck. Lucas's lawyer Tom Pollock, who years later became the chief of Universal Pictures, made a deal with science fiction publishing guru Judy-Lynn del Rey at Ballantine Books to publish the *Star Wars* novelization, the script, and a book about the making of the film, which later ended up at Random House as a children's book. The following month, the Fox board of directors—all of whom were given a black vinyl portfolio filled with photographic reproductions of Ralph McQuarrie's paintings and Joe Johnston's line drawings—gave the final go-ahead for filming, although one director said he hated the title and asked that it be changed. (It was. *The* was dropped.) ⚡ Fox corporate directors weren't the only ones with doubts. In early January, Lippincott did a slide presentation before a major Fox sales convention attended by theater owners. The theme was "26 [films] in '76," although *Star Wars* wouldn't open until May 1977. He received plaudits from Fox's head of international distribution and a few junior exhibition executives. "Most of the rest of the theater owners were ho-hum about it; they really thought it sounded pretty boring," Lippincott says. The exhibitors voted with their wallets.

Jim Rumpf's Chewbacca Mug for California Originals was one of the earliest and nicest items to come from the first film. It remains a George Lucas favorite. An R2-D2 mug with a hinged dome was also contemplated but dropped in the prototype stage for fear of banging too many little fingers.

An R2-D2 cookie jar seemed a natural because of R2's shape, and here it is— as translated by Roman Ceramics.

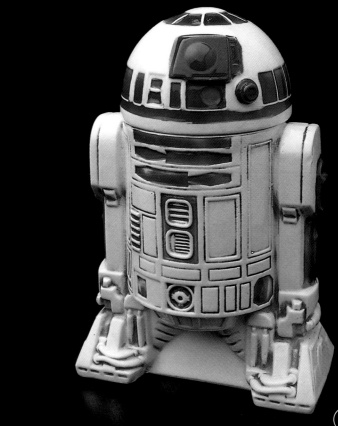

Art by Howard Chaykin for the first-ever Star Wars *poster. Lucasfilm didn't have much success selling them at $1 each. Now they go for several hundred dollars.*

When it came time for them to bid on the film—basically to offer advance guarantees—*Star Wars* brought in only $1.5 million, just fifteen percent of what Fox executives had expected. After all, theater owners reasoned, the science fiction genre had been dead for years. ⚡ Lippincott got a similar reception when he went to New York to try to interest Marvel Comics in doing a *Star Wars* miniseries to start several months before the film came out. Publisher Stan Lee told him, "Come see me when you're finished with your film." Refusing to take no for an answer, Lippincott met with Marvel contributing editor Roy Thomas, and over a spaghetti dinner filled him in on the story, showed him the McQuarrie paintings, and asked him to handle the comic book adaptation of *Star Wars* along with artist Howard Chaykin. Thomas was hooked and used his considerable powers of persuasion on Lee. The comic book became one of Marvel's most successful titles and lasted for 107 issues over nine years. ⚡ Wearing his promotional hat, Lippincott came up with the concept of attending fan conventions to talk up *Star Wars*, a technique that led to huge opening-day crowds and which became standard for fantasy and horror films. The first and biggest gathering was the annual San Diego comic convention in the summer of 1976, an affair that draws fans and comics professionals from all over the U.S. Chaykin and Thomas spoke about the upcoming comic series, and Lippincott asked convention goers what model kits and toy lines they liked best, and what kinds of merchandise they might be interested in buying. ⚡ The first limited *Star Wars* collectibles were available in San Diego. There were T-shirts with the movie's initial triangular logo, badges with the film's name, and a special poster drawn by Chaykin, marked "*Star Wars* Corporation Poster #1." Only one

BELOW:
A very limited edition Jawa plush doll, available only in Canada, was made by Regal Toy Limited of Toronto.

thousand were printed and offered at $1 each to cover costs. Most were left by the end of the convention. Today they sell for $400 and up. ⚡ For its part, Fox at first didn't seem to know what to do about merchandising. The job belonged to an executive whose main function was to oversee the studio's backlot. Then Fox wanted to bring in an outside licensing agent, but Lucasfilm objected because the agent represented a potentially competing science fiction property. Finally, Fox attorney Marc Pevers, who oversaw contracts and was involved in Fox's successful *Planet of the Apes* licensing, made his move to fill the vacuum. So Lippincott and Pevers hitched their wagon to *Star Wars* and rode it for all it was worth. It was, and remains, the most successful movie merchandising campaign in history. ⚡ The first mass-market item, the Ballantine paperback *Star Wars* novelization by George Lucas, came out in December 1976, and sold out its first printing of 125,000 in less than three months—quite a respectable showing for a "new author." Lippincott tried to persuade Ballantine to reprint the novel, but the publisher decided to wait until the movie opened to see if that would be worthwhile. It was. In the last fifteen years, more than five million paperbacks have been printed worldwide, including translations ranging from Finnish to Hungarian. ⚡ December also brought the first theatrical trailer or preview for the film—somewhat unusual six months before it was scheduled to open. Even more unusual was the fact that two trailers had been made—one ordered by Fox and one made by a TV commercial producer picked by Lucasfilm. The choice was Alan Ladd's—and he picked Lucasfilm's. The trailer was accompanied by the first full-sized theatrical poster, an expensive, shiny black-and-silver mylar sheet that announced in bold letters, "COMING TO YOUR GAL-

> ➤ STAR WARS FACTOID ≺

Perhaps the strangest copyright infringement case involving *Star Wars* revolved around rock singer-songwriter Neil Young. In late 1978, creatures appearing to all the world (and to the *Los Angeles Times* pop music critic) as Jawas started appearing on stage with Young during a concert tour and then in a tour film, on an album called *Rust Never Sleeps*, and in advertising—including a huge billboard on Los Angeles's Sunset Strip. Rather than get into an extended legal battle, lawyers for Young agreed to settle the case out of court. It was never clear what the Jawas were doing with Young in the first place.

A couple of Jawas setting out to do some scavenging, no doubt.

AXY THIS SUMMER." It was then that Lippincott and Pevers sent out letters to several hundred manufacturers telling them that the film would be a spectacular licensing vehicle as well as a great movie and a major event, but the response was negligible. ⚡ Clearly, the key to any long-term merchandising success would be toys. Because toys are a highly visible, mass-market item as opposed to limited edition collectibles or even peripheral items such as gum cards, a great toy line could bring in hefty revenues and help promote the film and any sequels. The trick was finding the right company; for a while, the trick seemed to be finding *any* company. ⚡ A few small manufacturers offered to make a single game, or a series of cheap, bagged plastic toys with a paper *Star Wars* logo slapped on, but Lucasfilm wouldn't entertain such offers. With the film premiere less than four months away, Lippincott and Pevers traveled to New York in February 1977 to attend Toy Fair, the annual trade show where manufacturers show their lines for the year to toy retailers. The men set up a slide show at Fox New York headquarters and made the rounds trying to get toy makers to at least look at and listen to their pitch. At one company that had past ties to Fox, a top executive literally shoved Lippincott out the door of his office. ⚡ But one toy company not only expressed interest in *Star Wars*, but had the resources to follow through. Kenner Products, founded in Cincinnati in 1947, was bought by General Mills, the big cereal maker, twenty years later. Kenner's first product was a seasonal outdoor toy, the Bubble-Gun. It went on to make a staple out of Play-Doh modeling compound, scored with its Baby Alive doll, and hit it big with a line based on the popular *Six Million Dollar Man* television series. ⚡ But would Kenner risk developing a toy line based on a science fiction film filled with aliens and robots with strange-sounding names, all being controlled by something mystical called the Force? If *Star Wars* had taken one visionary to bring the story to life on film, it took another to reduce the characters to under four inches high and bring them to the children of the world. George Lucas's counterpart in the toy world was Kenner president Bernard Loomis, and fortuitously, he was on the lookout for the next hot toy. ⚡ In late January, Pevers had talked on the telephone to Craig Stokely, Kenner's vice-president, product planning, and had gotten a positive enough response to send him a follow-up letter with a copy of the script and a portfolio of stills and drawings from the film. What Pevers and Lippincott couldn't have known was that, inside Kenner, several top designers were salivating over the prospect of becoming part of Lucas's universe.

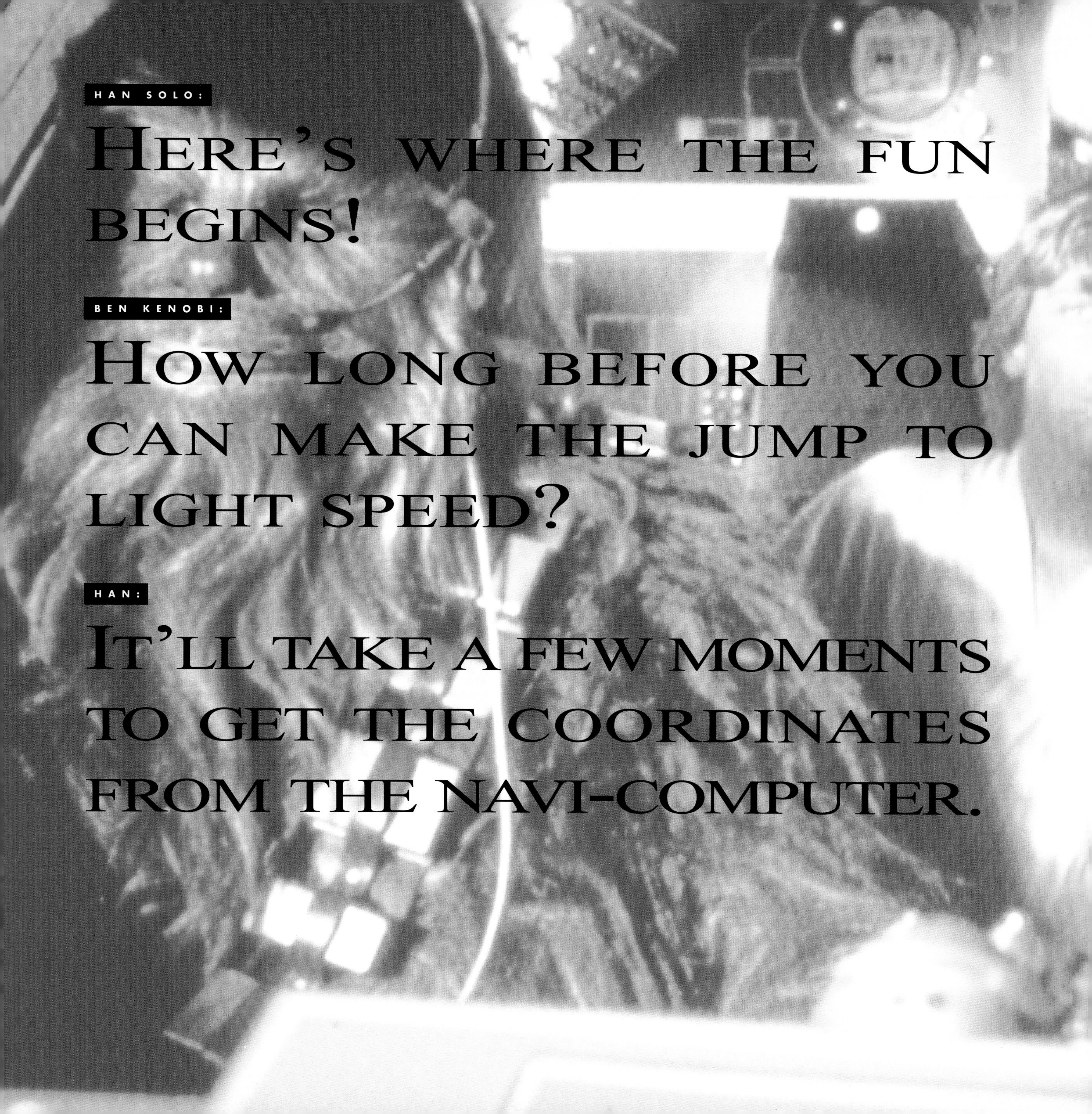

HAN SOLO:

HERE'S WHERE THE FUN BEGINS!

BEN KENOBI:

HOW LONG BEFORE YOU CAN MAKE THE JUMP TO LIGHT SPEED?

HAN:

IT'LL TAKE A FEW MOMENTS TO GET THE COORDINATES FROM THE NAVI-COMPUTER.

LUKE SKYWALKER:

ARE YOU KIDDING? AT THE RATE THEY'RE GAINING...

HAN:

TRAVELING THROUGH HYPERSPACE ISN'T LIKE DUSTING CROPS, BOY!

—*STAR WARS*

CHAPTER

PROPHETIC AND TOYETIC

Early in 1977, Bernie Loomis was reading *The Hollywood Reporter* when a squib caught his eye. It mentioned an upcoming space movie from Fox called *Star Wars*. From that moment, and for the next twelve months, Loomis and his colleagues were caught up in as harrowing, yet exhilarating an adventure as any that enmeshed Luke Skywalker and Han Solo. Their enemies were time and rip-off artists, who tried to make a quick buck off the *Star Wars* phenomenon by selling such things as cheap

flashlights with plastic tubes and calling them lightsabers. ⚡ Loomis, president of Kenner Products, was already a legend in the toy industry, both admired for his instincts and disliked by some for his brash manner, but always willing to take risks. Loomis doesn't pretend to be a Hollywood seer. "Nobody could've predicted how big the movie would become," he says. "In fact, I assumed the film would come and go quickly—movies never lasted more than a couple of months—and that we'd do the toys the following year without any movie there to help us." Fox did hold out the possibility that *Star Wars* would become a weekly television series, much like *Planet of the Apes*, and the initial deal was structured to provide higher royalties for a TV series than for the film. ⚡ Kenner felt comfortable with licensed properties. It had done well with *Six Million Dollar Man* and was counting on another license to be as big: the upcoming TV series, *Man from Atlantis*. Loomis also felt *Star Wars* had certain "toyetic" qualities, so he bargained hard and got exclusive worldwide rights for all toy-related products. That actually worked to the long-term benefit of the *Star Wars* license, because it kept schlock merchandise off the shelves and made sure that an avalanche of product didn't flatten the market all at once, a problem that led to the relatively short shelf life of toys from an even higher-grossing film, *E.T. The Extra-Terrestrial*. ⚡ If Loomis was merely intrigued by *Star Wars*, the toy designers at Kenner, many of whom were downright passionate about getting the license, had been George Lucas fans since *THX 1138* and *American Graffiti*. In fact, *THX 1138* had been one of toy designer Jim Swearingen's favorite movies in college, and he had read a small blurb about Lucas's new science fiction movie in *Starlog* magazine. In addition to Swearingen—who designed Kenner's first

two vehicles, the X-Wing and TIE Fighter—the design team, headed by David Okada, vice-president of preliminary design, included Tom Osborne and Mark Boudreaux, a University of Cincinnati industrial design major who started working at Kenner in a work-study program just as the *Star Wars* line was being launched. ⚡ The designers' enthusiasm grew as they saw more from the film. Some of Kenner's marketing staff weren't so sure, but once Bernie Loomis gave the go-ahead, the design staff went into overdrive. In fact, Okada was so enthusiastic that Loomis had to cap his effervescence during several tough negotiating sessions that led to a final agreement with Fox and Lucasfilm in April 1977. ⚡ Contractually, Kenner promised only to market one "all-family action board game" in 1977 and said it "contemplated" selling three different action playsets with figures the following year. But behind the scenes, the design department was cooking on all burners. ⚡ "We went nuts," Okada remembers. "We worked around the clock to come up with ideas and prototypes to present to Fox and Lucas, who had the right of final approval on everything. I was so excited the day the preliminary agreement was reached that I went home, dug into my sock drawer, and pulled out a tan sock to make a doll of one of the sand people and a brown sock to make a Jawa. We had model kits of tanks all over the office that we were bashing to make prototype vehicles." ⚡ The key decision in the launch of the *Star Wars* line—one that not only ensured its success but has influenced the toy industry to this day—was made in Loomis's office early one morning just as the March sun was rising over Cincinnati. Okada was in his office when Loomis called a little after 7 A.M. and asked him to come upstairs. ⚡ Kenner had been successful with twelve-inch-tall

OPPOSITE PAGE:
After an original drawing and preliminary model are made, someone draws the pattern. This is an engineering layout for the X-Wing Fighter.

PAGE 61:
Kenner's Ewok Village Action Playset.

ABOVE:
An X-Wing Fighter toy prepares to take on the Death Star for the umpteenth time.

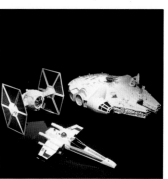

RIGHT:
Kenner's first three toy vehicles were the most important ones in all three films: The TIE Fighter, X-Wing Fighter, and Millennium Falcon.

A Stormtrooper rides a Patrol Dewback on Tatooine.

Six Million Dollar Man dolls, as Hasbro had been with G.I. Joe. But *Star Wars* was clearly going to be a vehicle- and accessory-driven line, and if a twelve-inch Han Solo was going to pilot his Millennium Falcon, the ship would have to be five feet in diameter and cost several hundred dollars. That was clearly impossible. ⚡ "We were hashing it around," Okada says, "trying to decide what to do, when Bernie held up his right hand, the thumb and forefinger apart, and asked, "How about that big, Dave?" The designer took a six-inch steel ruler from his shirt pocket, measured the open space at three-and-three-quarter inches, and the two men decided that would be as good a height as any for the hero, Luke Skywalker, with the other figures scaled from there. ⚡ This decision also enabled Kenner to score on the collectibility front. While marketers at first thought kids would choose

from among their favorite characters, it turned out that at under $2 a figure, they wanted them all—a line that would grow to 111 different figures by 1985. The size of the figures also led to reasonable prices for the vehicles and playsets, since they could be much smaller. ⚡ To keep costs down, the figures didn't have twisting waists or bendable knees, and that led to some problems. When Kenner produced a Patrol Dewback, a green dinosaurlike creature ridden by Stormtroopers in the Tatooine desert, the designers couldn't figure out how to sit a figure astride the Dewback. An early design had a strange-looking saddle with protruding holsterlike appendages for a figure's feet. "Then someone tried a trap door in the top of the Dewback, so the figure could stand, but look like it was sitting," Okada says. "It was bizarre, it was hokey, but it looked okay, so Lucasfilm said yes." ⚡ The initial game

FROM LEFT TO RIGHT:

TOP ROW:
Imperial Stormtrooper, Rebel Soldier, Princess Leia Organa, Obi Wan Kenobi, Han Solo, Star Destroyer Commander, FX-7, Hammerhead, Walrus Man, Tusken Raider, IG-88, R5-D4, Ugnaught, Jawa, Power Droid, Yoda, Luke Skywalker (X-Wing Fighter Pilot), Death Star Droid, Bossk.

SECOND ROW:
Luke Skywalker, AT-AT Driver, Han Solo (Bespin), Lando Calrissian, C-3PO, Greedo, Princess Leia (Bespin), Rebel Commander, Lobot, Han Solo (Hoth), AT-AT Commander, Boba Fett, Chewbacca, Bespin Security Guard, 2-1B, Snaggletooth, Dengar, Imperial Commander, Luke Skywalker (Bespin), Stormtrooper (Hoth).

THIRD ROW:
Princess Leia (Hoth), Luke Skywalker (Hoth), Bespin Security Guard, 4-LOM, Darth Vader, Cloud Car Pilot, Zuckuss, Imperial TIE Fighter Pilot, Admiral Ackbar, Lando Calrissian (Skiff Guard), Chief Chirpa, Weequay, Logray, Ree-Yees, Rebel Commando, Nien Numb, General Madine, Gamorrean Guard, Biker Scout.

FOURTH ROW:
8D8, Han Solo (Trench Coat), Prune Face, Princess Leia (Combat Poncho), Klaatu (Skiff Guard), Wicket W. Warrick, Bib Fortuna, Rancor Keeper, Luke Skywalker (Jedi Knight), AT-ST Driver, The Emperor, Emperor's Royal Guard, Klaatu, Princess Leia (Boushh), Nikto, B-Wing Pilot, Teebo, Squid Head.

FIFTH ROW:
EV-9D9, R2-D2, Han Solo (Carbonite), Warok, Imperial Dignitary, Romba, Barada, Lando Calrissian (General Pilot), Anakin Skywalker, Luke Skywalker (Stormtrooper), Imperial Gunner, Luke Skywalker (Battle Poncho), A-Wing Pilot, Paploo, Amanaman, Lumat.

they didn't shoot bullets, and I don't think you ever saw any blood."
⚡ Turning film props into toys is a lot more difficult than it seems. "The advantage the film people had was that nothing had to work; they could fudge everything," Jim Swearingen notes. "We had to make compromises for reasons of playability, durability, and safety, so the toy vehicles had to be a little chunkier and a little less elegant than their movie counterparts." ⚡ Many of the small action figures went through changes too. Loomis wanted Luke Skywalker's lightsaber to appear "magically" in his hand. One prototype Luke had a knob in his back that was used to crank a lightsaber made of heavy monofilament (like a very sturdy fishing line) out from Luke's hand and then back again. But because it wound on an internal spool, the lightsaber tended to come out curved, and the concept was abandoned. The first Luke actually manufactured had a hard plastic lightsaber embedded in his arm that telescoped twice, but it was complicated and expensive to produce, so later versions were changed to a lightsaber that telescoped once. Subsequent Lukes, dressed in different costumes, had snap-on weapons. ⚡ Heroic Han Solo underwent some sculpting changes; his original pinhead was out of proportion to his muscular body. The tiny Jawa, one of the smallest figures in the line, went from wearing a vinyl cape to a somewhat richer-looking cloth cape in an attempt to add perceived value to the figure, which cost the same as its larger counterparts. Today, of course, scarcity makes a collectible, and the vinyl-caped Jawa sells for several hundred dollars. ⚡ There were also the inevitable mistakes because of time pressures and misinformation. Kenner's special Cantina Adventure Set included a full-sized Snaggletooth wearing gloves and boots, but the creature's size and look were a guess, since the only photo given Kenner showed the creature cut off at the waist. Actually, Snaggletooth was a dwarf with hairy hands and paws, and the figure had to be resculpted. ⚡ Perhaps the most important action figure change took place before production. The figure of the fierce bounty hunter Boba Fett, who appeared in the televised *Star Wars Christmas Special* and was supposed to have a major role in *The Empire Strikes Back*, was used as a mail-in promotional offer. He was widely advertised as having a spring-loaded, missile-firing backpack. But shortly before the first figure was to ship, rival Mattel Toys had a widely publicized product recall of vehicles from *Battlestar Galactica* because similar missiles had injured young children. Kenner quickly put stickers over all Boba Fett packaging and signage that had touted

LEFT:
The original full-sized acetate sculptings of the rare Yak Face (by Bill Lemon), Darth Vader and C-3PO (both by John Gardner) next to the final produced figures.

RIGHT:
The original vinyl-caped Jawa action figure was replaced by the one with a cloth cape shortly after production began. Guess which is more valuable today!

late fall, but despite its best efforts, the company wouldn't be able to ship any action figures or vehicles by Christmas. Other manufacturers, many of them fly-by-night, took advantage by shipping millions of cheap lightsaber-like toys or used old molds and repackaged ten-year-old space toys. ⚡ Kenner was getting bad publicity. Even worse, it was losing big money. That's when Bernie Loomis thought up the empty-box-for-Christmas gambit. "I decided to give the kids a pretty picture and a promise to their parents that we'd deliver the toys as soon as possible after Christmas," Loomis says. "Everybody at Kenner tried to talk me out of it." The certificate packages, which were sealed tighter than Fort Knox to prevent in-store pilferage, contained a thin cardboard "stage" for the first twelve action figures, a few assorted pieces of paper, and a certificate redeemable by mail for the first four action figures. Some six-hundred-thousand were shipped. A large number went unsold and were returned by retailers after Christmas, and the concept was knocked in the press and by some television commentators. But the certificates reminded the public that Kenner *Star Wars* toys were on the way, and thus were a marketing success. ⚡ A few children, however, received a set of *Star Wars* action figures before Christmas. In November 1977, Loomis was in Monte Carlo for a Monopoly tournament, and the Fox board of directors was meeting at a nearby hotel. Loomis took the opportunity to show Kenner's upcoming *Star Wars* line to the directors. ⚡ "I told them that I had the very first early production set of figures and I was going to draw one of their names and give it to that person as a gift," Loomis recalls. "Of course, the drawing was rigged." Loomis presented the set to Fox's most famous—and certainly most attractive—director, Princess Grace of Monaco, the for-

mer actress Grace Kelly. "She told me she'd be very popular at home that night," Loomis laughs. ⚡ Princess Grace may have had the first set, but some 250 million small action figures followed in the next eight years, bought by children all over the world.

The battered bounty hunter droid, IG-88, is the largest and rarest of the Kenner dolls and was the last in the line. Here the final gray doll stands next to an earlier "hard copy" from which the engineers decided on final changes before the molds were made.

ASTEROIDS!

OH, NO! CHEWIE, SET TWO-SEVEN-ONE.

WHAT ARE YOU DOING? YOU'RE NOT ACTUALLY GOING INTO AN ASTEROID FIELD?

THEY'D BE CRAZY TO FOLLOW US, WOULDN'T THEY?

LEIA: You don't have to do this to impress me.

C-3PO: Sir, the possibility of successfully navigating an asteroid field is approximately three thousand, seven hundred and twenty to one.

HAN: Never tell me the odds!

—THE EMPIRE STRIKES BACK

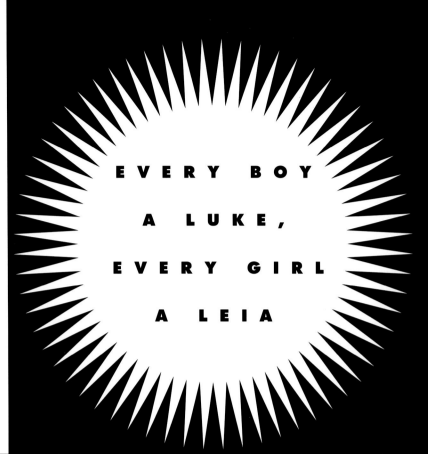

**EVERY BOY
A LUKE,
EVERY GIRL
A LEIA**

Mark Boudreaux's jaw dropped. A college student majoring in industrial design, he had just started a three-month work-study assignment at Kenner Products. Along with the rest of the design staff, he had been ushered into a conference room to have lunch and watch a brief trailer for an upcoming movie. It was, of course, the trailer for *Star Wars*, and the designers started pounding on the table in excitement. For the next eight years, Boudreaux was to have a leading role in what he calls "a fantasy

come true," turning the *Star Wars* trilogy into one of the most successful toy lines ever. ⚡ The toy business has a number of similarities to the movie business. They are somewhat fad-driven. They often rely on skillful marketing. After huge sums of money are spent up-front, they depend on public acceptance after the product is already made. And they have huge supporting casts behind the scenes. In fact, even George Lucas notes that many of the toy makers at Kenner could easily have changed places with their creative counterparts at Industrial Light & Magic. "The people at Kenner were real designers and craftsmen," he says. ⚡ In the initial frenzy at Kenner to get *something* out the door, not everything worked. "One of the first things we shipped was a boxed puzzle that had so much black sky and so many small stars, that it was almost impossible to put together," says Jim Black, the product manager. "But we had only twelve different slides to work with. Anyhow, the puzzles were very popular and our problems didn't seem to matter to the people who loved *Star Wars*." ⚡ Kenner hadn't been in the business of producing board games, but instead of giving a piece of the action to its affiliate, Parker Bros., it decided to try its own hand. The results looked fine, although the playability wasn't always high. One concept that didn't make it past the prototype stage sounds niftier than some games that were produced. It was a three-dimensional game with an eight-inch-diameter plastic Death Star in the center. The Death Star had a "sweet spot," and at the corners of the game were four X-Wing Fighters on flexible support rods. Hit the right spot with an X-Wing, and the Death Star "exploded." ⚡ Lots of other prototypes never went into production: a detailed, foot-tall, tethered remote-control R2-D2 with compartments that opened and other

moving pieces; a pull-string talking Yoda that spoke in his movie voice; a twelve-inch Lando Calrissian doll that looked like Billy Dee Williams; C-3PO walkie-talkies; a small action figure of Gargan, the six-breasted harridan who danced in Jabba the Hutt's throne room; and Jedi and Boba Fett role-play outfits—child-size plastic accessories to turn kids into a hero or bounty hunter. ⚡ Some concepts got as far as the full-scale model stage, or were even photographed for Kenner's annual catalog for the retail trade. Catalogs produced for Kenner's Canadian, British, French, and other affiliates went to press even sooner and had photos of early prototypes of *Star Wars* toys, some bearing little resemblance to the finished product, such as a Lando Calrissian doll that's really a Kenner *Hardy Boys* doll with a brown face. ⚡ Why weren't certain toys produced? Sometimes internal cost auditors said a toy

CLOCKWISE FROM ABOVE:
Kenner development sketch for a talking Yoda doll, book, and cassette that were never produced.

Pre-production, machine–molded Talking Yoda. Pull the string and it says six different phrases in Yoda's distinctive voice such as, "Beware the dark side!" and "So certain are you?" Despite the effort that went into its making, the doll never was produced and only two copies are known to exist today.

Early hand-sculpted Yoda prototype talking doll.

OPPOSITE PAGE:
"Escape from Death Star" games from Italy, Germany, Japan, and the United States.

PAGE 75:
Prototype costumes for 12" Luke and Leia dolls.

LEFT:
Prototype of a never-produced 12-inch doll of Lando Calrissian— in a perfect likeness of Billy Dee Williams—accompanied by Han Solo and Luke Skywalker decked out in proposed Hoth and Bespin outfits, respectively, from The Empire Strikes Back. *The clothing was designed and made by Kenner's Jane Abbott.*

RIGHT:
Kenner considered selling "role play" sets to let youngsters act out various characters using full-size props. Here are two design proposals from Mark Boudreaux for bounty hunter and Jedi Knight sets.

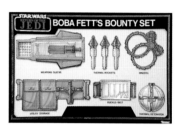

would cost too much to make, and thus would be too expensive to sell. Or the marketing staff was negative on a toy's prospects. Some planned line extensions, such as the large Lando doll and additional Micro Collection miniature playsets, weren't produced because the initial items didn't sell well. And major retailers sometimes said they simply weren't interested in carrying a particular toy. ⚡ Kenner resisted the urge to slap *Star Wars* labels on everything in sight, but there were some such products in the early days. Luke Skywalker's headset radio was a *Six Million Dollar Man* design, but molded in black plastic instead of blue. A large, expensive, and failure-prone arcade-like game, the X-Wing Aces Target Game, was a slight variation of an earlier Aerial Aces target game. (Much later, Kenner borrowed from *Star Wars*, using molds from a number of Ewok toys to produce *Robin Hood: Prince*

of Thieves toys in 1991.) ⚡ Designing the *Star Wars* toy universe went beyond capturing a certain look. "Knowing what the vehicles did in the film was as important as having the photographs to work from," Mark Boudreaux explains. "We had to know, for example, how the Millennium Falcon was used so we could build in compartments where some of the heroes could hide, and have space for Luke to fire the laser cannon or for Chewbacca and R2-D2 to play a holographic chess game." ⚡ Most of the vehicles needed to be reproportioned as well as rescaled from the ILM models, but the Kenner designers did the work so artfully that the changes aren't readily apparent. The designers started with a vehicle's cockpit, which had to fit at least one action figure. Boudreaux used a Chewbacca figure—then the tallest in the line— that had been cut in half lengthwise. He'd project a photograph

*A flurry of activity seems to
be taking place inside and around
Kenner's most popular ship, the
Millennium Falcon. The removable
rear-section top piece gives
easy access to hidden chambers and
a "holographic" chess game.*

Sometimes Kenner designers had to worry about details that the prop makers didn't have to contend with. Take the AT-ATs (All Terrain Armored Transports), the giant snow walkers used by the Imperial forces in the fierce battle at the start of *The Empire Strikes Back*. The Kenner designers needed a way for kids to put their mini-action figures inside the AT-ATs, so they asked the filmmakers about what appeared on photos to be a small exit underneath the walker's body. "It is not a door at the bottom, but a small hatch," replied Lucasfilm vice-president Carol Titelman. "There is *no* determination of how characters get in or out of the AT-AT. It may always remain a mystery!" The toy designers came up with their own solution: a removable side hatch.

ABOVE LEFT:
Layout and engineering drawings, "scrap" photos from Lucasfilm, decal placement illustrations, final package design—a lot went into the development of one of Kenner's largest toys, the Imperial Shuttle.

BELOW LEFT:
Han Solo in his Hoth battle gear comforts Princess Leia and the droids as he mounts his trusty Tauntaun and sets out to find the missing Luke Skywalker before nightfall.

The All Terrain Armored Transport
(AT-AT) or Imperial Walker,
was one of the Emperor's
most feared weapons. Here it's been
transported to Endor and used
to act out a face-off that never took
place on screen.

of a vehicle on a piece of paper and enlarge it until its cockpit fit his sliced Chewbacca. But if the rest of the ship, say an X-Wing or Falcon, were drawn in the same proportions, it would become too big and too expensive. So the designers shrunk fuselages and made wings shorter to get the right dimensions for a toy.

⚡ Boudreaux and the other designers would take the photographs and whatever other information they could get from Lucasfilm, and start sketching. The initial photographs were mounted on cardboard, and line drawings would be done if the photos weren't distinct enough. "We'd discuss what the features would be, based on what the ship did in the film, determine how big it would be, based on the action figures, and estimate how much it might cost," Boudreaux says. The visual images would be presented at a monthly Kenner meeting, and a cardboard model would be ready for the next meeting. "Then we'd go through our costing stage, draw an exploded view of the toy, and get involved with engineering, which would tell us what kind of plastic we needed to use, depending upon a part's complexity." The engineering department would also make up "bread boards," working models of just the electronic or mechanical action features on the toys.

⚡ Occasionally some secondary features would be removed at the costing stage to reduce the vehicle's price. Then it was time for the internal "turnover." The preliminary designers would package up all photos, drawings, costing information, and any cardboard or plastic models, and turn them over to the production designers and engineers. ⚡ Next, the production designers would determine specifics such as colors and label design, while engineering would make detailed drawings of each piece of the toy, making

The Y-Wing Fighter was a battlehorse for the fierce Mon Calamari people led by Admiral Ackbar—shown here at the helm of the Kenner toy.

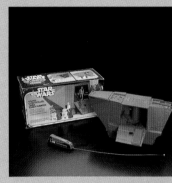

sure they would all be able to stand up to mass production of hundreds of thousands of units or more; the engineering department would add the complex patterns and scribed lines that are key to the look of *Star Wars* vehicles. These were then translated into beautifully handcrafted wood models, usually twice the size of the final toy to get in as much detailing as possible. Outside vendors then used the wooden forms to cut steel molds that pressed out the toy's plastic parts. A mold was made to exact size in a process called pantography, which traces the original model with a stylus connected to reducing gears and a tool that cuts the steel.

⚡ Depending on particular needs, up to a dozen handmade prototypes of some of the toys were made to photograph for catalogs or packaging, or for sales or other presentations. There would also be "first shots," unpainted toy pieces that were pressed by

➤ **STAR WARS FACTOID** ◄

Among the rarest manufactured merchandise with an official nod were a handful of items produced by Kenner-sponsored Junior Achievement groups. Among the items sold by the youngsters in the groups, usually in quantities of about five hundred: a *Star Wars* magnetic dart game; a *Star Wars* black plastic "message center" silkscreened with the film's logo; and an *Empire Strikes Back* character clock. Everything was approved by Kenner and Lucasfilm. But one Junior Achievement group in upstate New York produced an unauthorized *Star Wars III* board game that its creator then tried to peddle to Kenner. The toy company wasn't amused and blew the whistle.

The Rebels in a fierce battle against Imperial forces on Hoth, at least as envisioned by Kenner, which crammed no less than 14 toys into this shot. The low-flying cigar-shaped blimp is a Rebel Transport.

The Scout Walker, also dubbed the "Chicken Walker" for the anthropomorphic way it strutted, was another vehicle used by Imperial forces in defeating the Rebels on the ice planet Hoth. This is Kenner's version.

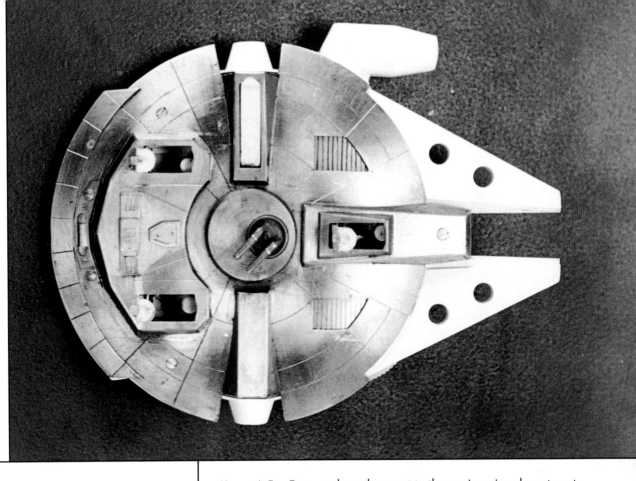

*Interior of Millennium Falcon toy
mock-up. Designer Mark Boudreaux
studied the* Star Wars *script to see
how the ship was used in order to
develop several "play scenarios."*

*Early Kenner model of the
Millennium Falcon; the smooth
surfaces give little hint of the
detailing to come.*

Kenner's Far East vendors, then sent to the engineering department for testing before final production began. ⚡ Some of the *Star Wars* toys, particularly the electronic ones, were developed by outside inventors. But nearly all the work was done in-house, and for Boudreaux at least, nothing was more satisfying than the series of mini-rigs that he developed from scratch. ⚡ As inflation and the skyrocketing price of plastic pushed up prices of even the simplest vehicles, the Kenner marketing department sought less expensive accessories for the action figures. So Boudreaux started designing one-man vehicles and body rigs that looked as if they *could* have been in the films, but maybe were just out of sight of the camera. ⚡ Ironically, the overwhelming consumer acceptance of Kenner's three-and-three-quarter-inch scale for articulated action figures, vehicles, and playsets led to the few failures in

If you didn't see any of these Mini-Rigs in the Star Wars films, that's because they were always "just out of camera range." That, anyhow, was the explanation of Kenner's Mark Boudreaux, who designed them all to provide lower-priced vehicles for the action figures.

The secret of Boudreaux's design for this Endor Forest Ranger as well as other low-priced mini-rigs, was that even though it didn't appear in any of the Star Wars *films, it looked like it could have. Plastic model by Nick Langdon based on Boudreaux's cardboard study model.*

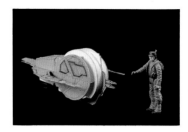

Sketches by Boudreaux show development of various mini-rig concepts.

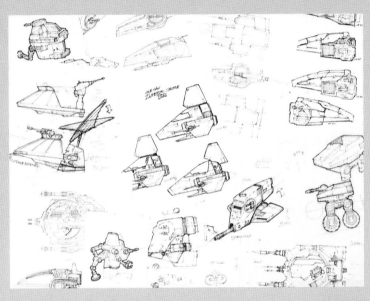

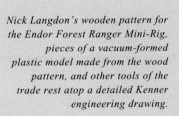

Nick Langdon's wooden pattern for the Endor Forest Ranger Mini-Rig, pieces of a vacuum-formed plastic model made from the wood pattern, and other tools of the trade rest atop a detailed Kenner engineering drawing.

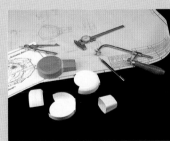

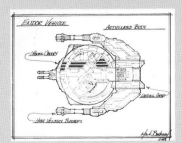

A design sketch by Boudreaux from a series that shows how his idea for an "Endor Bunker Blaster" evolved into the Endor Forest Ranger.

the *Star Wars* line. In the absence of matching vehicles, the twelve-inch dolls didn't have much play value, so a continuation of the line for *The Empire Strikes Back*—including new outfits for the main characters—was canceled. An even bigger disappointment was the attempt in the summer of 1982 to launch an entirely new scale of figures and playsets, the Micro Collection. The line was based on painted, die-cast metal figures that were about one-and-one-quarter-inches tall. Although each of the nine playsets and four vehicles came with anywhere from four to eight of the figures in various poses, they were on bases and couldn't be manipulated. The playsets were modular and fit together to make Bespin, Hoth, and Death Star "worlds," and plans were in the works for more vehicles and more worlds, including a miniature Ewok village.

⚡ Howard Bollinger, then vice-president, product design and engineering, says he originally conceived of the Micro line as more of a collectible than as a toy, with posed figures from dozens of major scenes in the films, along with diorama backgrounds.

⚡ The Kenner designers really threw themselves into the Micro Collection—literally. "We sat down and came up with ideas of what characters should go with each playset and what their poses should be," Boudreaux says. "Then we took all the furniture out of a large conference room, set up three cameras on tripods at different angles, and took turns being models, striking poses and using broom handles as lightsabers and other weapons. We gave those photos, along with photos of the characters, to sculptors who made the actual figures." ⚡ "Conceptually, the Micro Collection sounded like a clever idea," says David Mauer, who was Kenner's executive vice-president, marketing, at the time. "But, after the fact, we discovered that kids today hate posed soldier-like figures.

And the toys weren't open-ended. Once they put one of these Micro playsets on the ground, they were forced into a particular playing pattern, and by definition that's limiting." Also, many parents who had made a sizable investment in the larger scale toys were angered by what they saw as an attempt to force them into spending another pile of cash on an incompatible line. ⚡ Even the most successful toy line eventually loses steam, and by 1985 the *Star Wars* line was fading despite Kenner's best efforts. For one thing, an exhausted George Lucas had said publicly that *Return of the Jedi* would be the last film—at least for the foreseeable future. Attempts to do separate lines based on the short-lived *Droids* and *Ewoks* television cartoon series weren't very successful, perhaps because the main characters such as Han and Leia weren't present and the primal battle of good versus evil, Luke Skywalker versus Darth Vader, had been resolved. ⚡ Still, Mark Boudreaux and the other designers attempted to take the concept of the mini-rigs a logical step further by creating full-sized vehicles and characters that *might* have been in the *Star Wars* universe. There was a double-cockpit Tandem X-Wing Fighter; an XP-38 Land Speeder; an Imperial Outpost playset; and a dozen more for which elaborate drawings and scenarios were done. But Lucasfilm didn't want to go in that direction. ⚡ For many at Kenner, *Star Wars* was a once-in-a-lifetime experience. Mark Boudreaux remembers when kids in his neighborhood discovered that he was designing *Star Wars* toys. "I became like a god to them, and when I was able to give them a few of the toys before they were in the stores, I could do no wrong," he says. "The combination of George Lucas's films and Kenner toys made a whole lot of kids happy for a long time. It made some twenty-year-olds pretty happy too—one being myself."

➤ **S T A R   W A R S   F A C T O I D** ◄

The world that never was: Lucasfilm and Kenner got trademarks on more than 250 characters, vehicles, and "play environments," some of which never made it to the final toy stage. The list is tantalizing to today's collectors. It includes Light Brigade action playset; Mos Eisley Spaceport playset; Aunt Buru and Uncle Owen Lars toy action figures; Tatooine play environment; Tractor Beam action toy; Gaderffii Stick toy weapon; Bothan Spies; Dustbin robot; Great Pit of Carkoon playset; Planet Puff; and the Star Rattle.

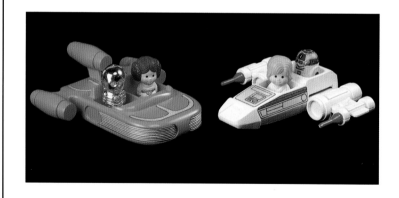

Lots of Kenner folks threw out ideas for new Star Wars *toys. Here is cost analyst Chet Wolgamot's concept for a preschool line. The Landspeeder and X-Wing are wood models and the baby-faced Leia, Luke, and the droids are hard-plastic, molded figures.*

In between battles, Luke and Leia could relax in these proposed outfits for the large dolls by Kenner's Jane Abbott.

If Kenner's large doll line had continued, Jane Abbott in the soft goods department was ready with these proposed outfits: three versions of a high-fashion Leia (the Leia meets Barbie look).

Mark Boudreaux's preliminary rendering of a modular Death Star tower and "throne room" was slated as an add-on to the Micro Death Star World playsets. It was never produced.

Kenner's Dave Tucker crafted this model of the Death Star addition out of cardboard and plastic. The Micro Collection wasn't a big seller and was canceled after just a year.

LEFT AND ABOVE:
The chill of the ice planet Hoth and the heat from Cloud City on the gaseous planet of Bespin can be felt in these Kenner photos of the interlocking toys that made up Hoth World and Bespin World. Each came with tiny, hand-painted metal figures in various action poses.

LEFT AND FAR LEFT:
Kenner designers and engineers had great hopes for the continuation of the Micro Collection, and were deep into development of several new miniature "worlds" when the line was canceled. Here are several model versions of the rejuvenation chamber on Hoth—dubbed the Bacta Chamber—where an injured Luke recovers, along with pattern drawings and a sample package.

ABOVE:
Development of a Micro Collection figure of Luke on a Tauntaun starts with Steve Varner's flesh-colored original wax sculpting. To ensure the proper detail, some toys are originally sculpted twice—or even four times—the size it will eventually be. A machine with reduction gears cuts the final mold from the larger hard-plastic figure. The final figure is then hand painted.

YOUR THOUGHTS BETRAY YOU, FATHER. I FEEL THE GOOD IN YOU...THE CONFLICT.

THERE IS NO CONFLICT.

YOU COULDN'T BRING YOURSELF TO KILL ME BEFORE, AND I DON'T BELIEVE YOU'LL DESTROY ME NOW.

You underestimate the power of the dark side. If you will not fight, then you will meet your destiny.

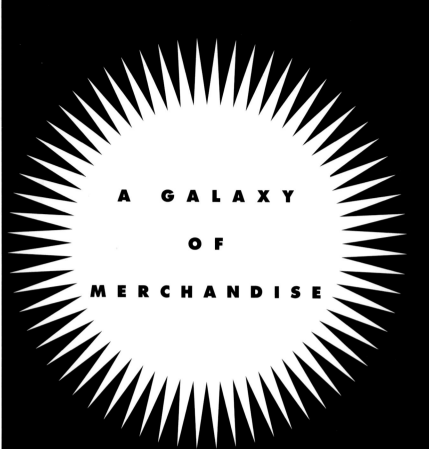

A GALAXY
OF
MERCHANDISE

Even the immediate public and critical acclaim for *Star Wars*, and the realization that the film would be a megahit, could hardly have prepared its creators for the movie's true destiny as a landmark in popular culture. But the signs were everywhere. In fact, they were on the chests of hundreds of thousands of men, women, and children who snapped up one of the few authorized items immediately available: T-shirts. The T-shirt transfers came from Factors Inc. in Bear, Delaware, a small firm that made its

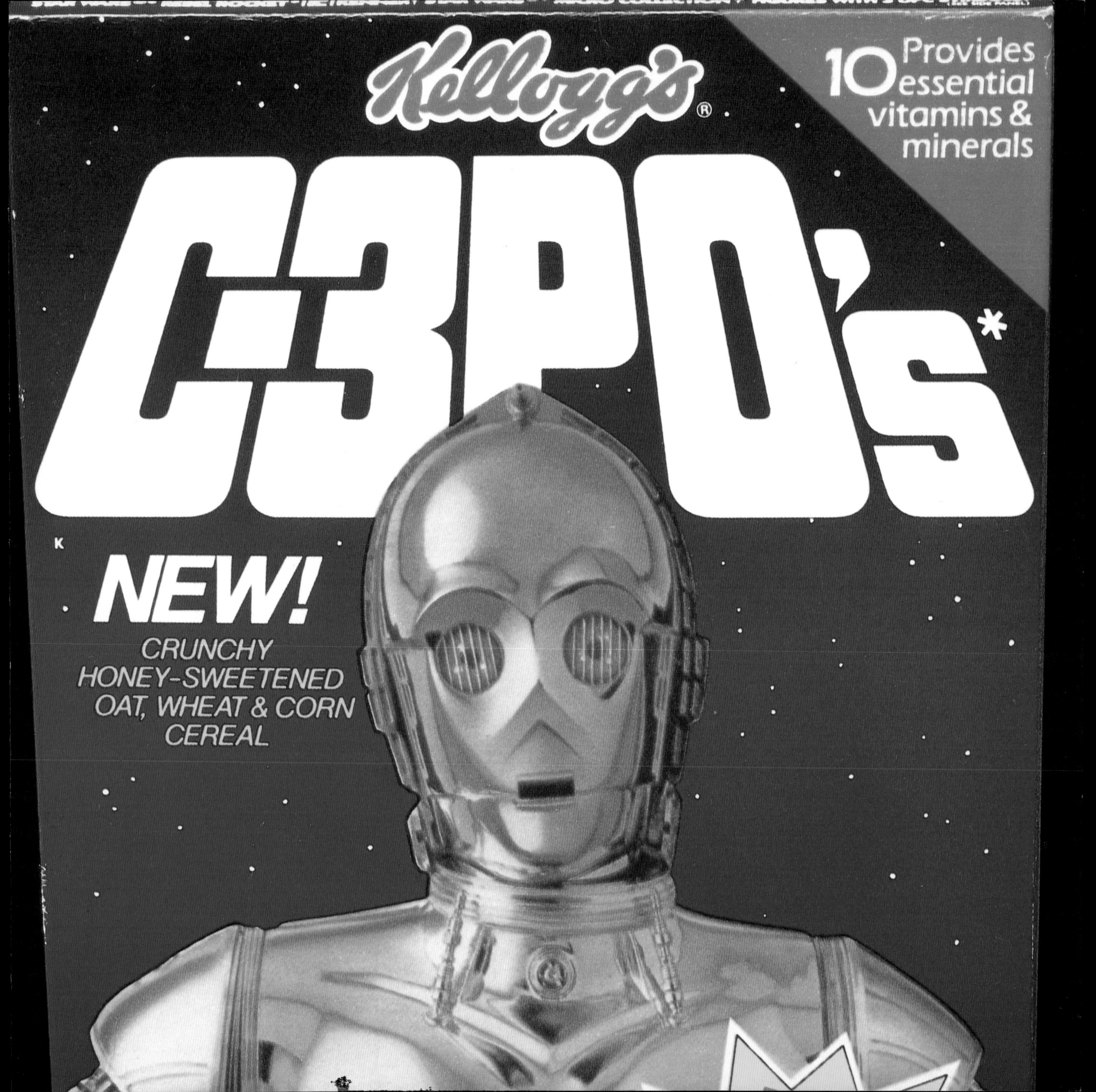
Kellogg's®
10 Provides essential vitamins & minerals
C3PO's*
K
NEW!
CRUNCHY
HONEY-SWEETENED
OAT, WHEAT & CORN
CEREAL

pre-*Star Wars* mark by selling millions of posters of Farrah Fawcett and Sylvester Stallone. Factors was one of the first firms on a list that grew to more than two hundred worldwide manufacturers who sold more than $2.5 billion worth of products tied to *Star Wars, Empire, Jedi, Droids, Ewoks, Star Tours,* and all their offspring. That list is still growing—*Star Wars* vitamins and Nintendo video games were added late in 1991—but Lucasfilm is awaiting the next three movies in the *Star Wars* epic cycle for a major push. ⚡ George Lucas puts the merchandising in perspective. "Nabisco sells more crackers than Hollywood sells movie tickets each year," he says. Yet, since merchandising provides royalties based on a small percentage of the wholesale value, the films themselves produced considerably more revenue for Lucasfilm than the merchandise. ⚡ In a way, having little product available in May 1977 probably helped the *Star Wars* merchandising phenomenon last as long as it did. For true consumer-driven demand, not some false sense of need created by a massive advertising campaign or hype, became what propelled the products. That changed somewhat by the time *The Empire Strikes Back* was released, and even more for *Return of the Jedi.* But by then, the new movies—which still built up a sense of great anticipation—had developed into something sort of comfortable. No matter how suspenseful and exciting *Empire* was, and how satisfying it was to have loose ends tied up in *Jedi,* nothing could recreate each moviegoer's original thrill at having *personally* discovered Luke, Leia, Han, and the rest of the crew. ⚡ "A lot of people don't like merchandising," Lucas concedes. "They don't like the idea of someone trading off one medium for another. But my feeling is that if you develop a fantasy world in a movie, it isn't a particularly

bad thing to have kids go home and be able to simulate a fantasy world there and continue to work through whatever emotional needs have been stirred by the film." As for charges that merchandising a film is just crass exploitation, Lucas points out that only one in ten movies ever makes much money, so filmmakers must try to get back what they can from a big hit. ⚡ At 20th Century Fox, Marc Pevers was given one marching order from movie chief Alan Ladd: "If Lucas doesn't want it, we won't license it." Pevers rejected some items without even checking with Lucasfilm's Charles Lippincott. "I turned down a ceramic liquor decanter in the shape of R2-D2," he says. "It wasn't the image we wanted for the film. You don't see liquor in a Mickey Mouse decanter. You can't cheapen characters that are part of Americana." ⚡ Some of the licensing requests were strange. "I remember a request from some professor who wanted to license a *Star Wars* light bulb," Pevers says. "He claimed it would be revolutionary. We passed." Also deep-sixed were *Star Wars* luggage—basically a suitcase with a label attached—and Darth Vader sunglasses, black and somewhat in the shape of the arch-villain's face mask. ⚡ Among the early major licensees was the Bibb Co., which had overwhelming success with its *Star Wars* line of sheets, pillow cases, blankets, bedspreads, sleeping bags, curtains, beach pads, beach towels, bathroom towels, and washcloths. Bibb did most of its bedding items in *eight* different designs: Galaxy, Space Fantasy, Lord Vader, and Jedi Knight; and special designs for Sears, J. C. Penney, Montgomery Ward, and Ratcliffe Bros. in England. And that was just for *Star Wars.* Bibb, like many of the other major licensees, signed on again for both sequels. ⚡ Don Post Studios, a small mask maker in North Hollywood, California, found its

Manufacturers constantly wanted to make Chewbacca the Wookiee fiercer than George Lucas intended. Lucas—who saw the character as an amalgam of bear, monkey, and Indiana, his Alaskan malamute dog—knew that beneath all that brown fur, Chewie was really a gentle soul. It was too late in the production cycle to do much about Kenner's fierce vampire-fanged fifty-inch inflatable Chewbacca bop bag (''Punch Chewbacca and he comes back for more''). But Don Post Studios' over-the-head masks were another matter. The first batch made Chewbacca look like first cousin to the Wolfman, with a protuberant nose and a wide, snarling mouth filled with pointy teeth. Close his mouth and make him gentler looking, Post was told. But some two hundred of the vicious Chewie masks were made and sold before the resculpted face could be produced, making at least some of today's collectors happy.

business explode overnight as it turned out authentic-looking over-the-head masks of six different characters, and then added to the line for the next two films. While the home Super 8-millimeter film business was in its twilight—on the eve of home video—Ken Films made its biggest killing ever by selling a few minutes of *Star Wars* excerpts on small plastic reels, especially in foreign markets where the movie hadn't yet opened. Even though only seven short snippets were licensed—enough to fill two small reels—the Italian distributor packaged them in seven different plastic boxes, five of which contained duplicate footage. ⚡ As successful as Factors, the T-shirt transfer company, was in some areas, it was also involved in what Lippincott calls two of the few fiascoes in *Star Wars* licensing. "They did a T-shirt transfer book with Ballantine, but the transfers were old and had already been out for a while,

Don Post Studios made 200 of the snarling Chewbacca masks before switching to the kinder, gentler variety at Lucasfilm's request.

Princess Leia was not only the dominant female character in the trilogy, but also the love interest. As toys, Leia figures could be used to draw girls to the *Star Wars* universe. Thus, Fundimensions set out to create a five-and-one-half-inch-tall white vinyl Leia figurine-to-paint for *The Empire Strikes Back*. The casting makes Leia look very stolid, her hair tightly braided, wearing a unisex snowsuit and packing a pistol. Some of the wags at Lucasfilm weren't impressed. While one wrote ''Wonderful!'' on an inner-office memo sheet that solicited comments on the prototype, another scrawled, ''Looks like George Washington.'' To which a second critic added, ''Maybe with paint, she'll look like Martha W.'' But Maggie Young, then head of merchandising, had the final word: ''She's prettier than a lot of *you*!''

and the book rotted on the shelves,'' he says. ''The other failure was the jewelry they sublicensed. We went back and forth on it, and we weren't too crazy about the concept, but eventually said yes. I think the whole charm bracelet fad had died, and I question whether girls wanted to put Darth Vader barrettes in their hair. But I think the main reason the jewelry didn't sell was that—to my eyes—it looked cheap.'' Still, the line grossed $3.5 million in a year. A more expensive line of jewelry in England—including a sterling silver *May the Force be With You* dog tag—fared much worse.

⚡ Lippincott says he wanted the surprise and sense of wonder from the film to carry over to the merchandise. But he admits to being a little bothered that the film's images of evil were taking over. ''The little kids went nuts over Darth Vader, and that really caught me off guard. But the film had a lot of other things going on. The younger girls fell for Luke, and the older ones for Han, and they all could fall in love with Chewbacca. Obi Wan was a father figure. And the science fiction nerd-type boys dreamed of Princess Leia. They even sent her marriage proposals.'' ⚡ The requests for domestic licenses flowed in. By 1979 there were *Star Wars* Halloween costumes and masks, overalls and jackets, digital and analog wristwatches, T-shirts, socks, shoes and sneakers and sandals, plastic tableware, greeting cards, gift wrap, a syndicated newspaper comic strip, flying rockets, plastic model kits, wallpaper, buttons and patches, lunch boxes, belts and buckles, jewelry, school supplies, ceramic mugs and banks and cookie jars, posters, gum trading cards, records and tapes, books and comics, pajamas and robes, sheets and towels—and, of course, lots of toys. ⚡ One licensed item brought in little money, but gave Lucasfilm a particular sense of pride. It was a *Star Wars* remedial reading kit

LEFT:
*A shelf display filled with
Bradley Time watches.*

RIGHT:
*One of the earliest Bradley Time
Star Wars wrist watches.
By* Return of the Jedi,
*Bradley had produced no fewer
than 30 different watches
and clocks for the United States
market alone.*

LEFT:
*"What R2-D2 is saying is that
you have to get up right away,"
C-3PO helpfully tells us,
translating his droid friend's
blips and beeps in this talking
alarm clock from Bradley Time.
"R2! You shouldn't be
so polite! This little Rebel is
going to be late!"*

CLOCKWISE FROM ABOVE:
*StrideRite did a line of children's
sneakers, boots, and shoelaces
for* Jedi.

*What every baby needs: fuzzy
Darth Vader booties manufactured
in Taiwan.*

*Imagine wheeling along
at hyperspeed on these beauties:
Darth Vader roller skates from
Brookfield Athletic Shoe Co.
For gentler types there were Wicket
the Ewok roller skates and for
northern types, ice skates.*

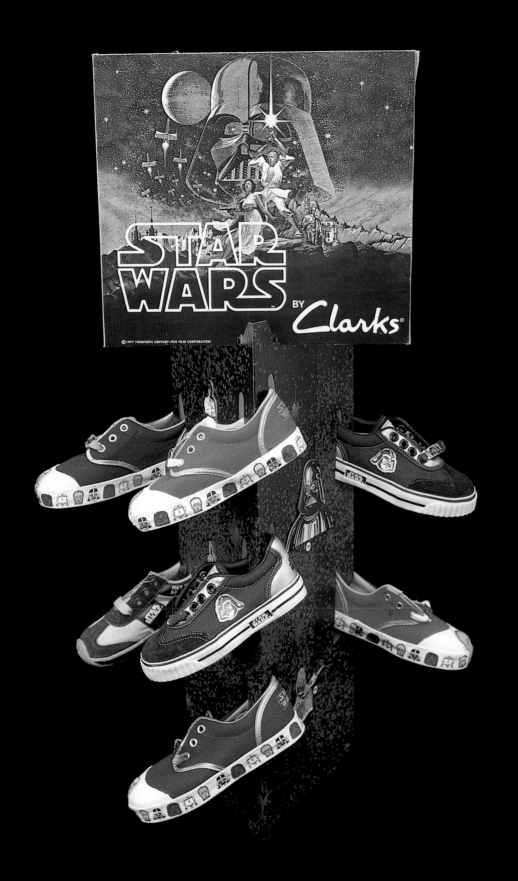

STAR WARS: FROM CONCEPT TO SCREEN TO COLLECTIBLE

OPPOSITE PAGE, ABOVE:
Ralph McQuarrie illustrated these
Lucasfilm Christmas cards.

OPPOSITE PAGE, BELOW:
More Lucasfilm Christmas card art
by McQuarrie. One illustration
(RIGHT) *also was used as the cover*
for the delightful Christmas in the
Stars *record album from RSO.*

ABOVE:
A McQuarrie illustration for a
"change of address" card for
Lucasfilm after it outgrew its small
offices because of the huge success
of Star Wars.

The Hamilton Collection issued this Star Wars *10th Anniversary china plate with 23k gold rim by artist Thomas Blackshear. It's slightly larger than the other eight plates that make up the set.*

CLOCKWISE FROM ABOVE, BOTTOM:

These three metal lunch boxes representing each film are the pick of the dozen made by the Thermos division of King-Seeley.

This unusual 14-piece badge set, available only to initial members of the Star Wars Fan Club, includes a photo of George Lucas among the characters he created.

These original crew patches were sewn onto jackets and caps of the filmmakers; some were later adapted and used as premiums for the Star Wars/Lucasfilm Fan Club.

Available soon after Star Wars opened were a set of solid brass belt buckles from Basic Tool & Supply Co. in Berkeley, CA. A clunkier-looking set was produced by The Leather Shop in San Francisco.

LEFT:
An Obi Wan Kenobi tankard sculpted by Jim Rumpf for California Originals.

RIGHT:
A large Darth Vader tankard seems more appropriate for shelf viewing than for downing a glass of cold milk.

OPPOSITE PAGE:
Roman Ceramics created small china banks of R2-D2, Darth Vader, and C-3PO.

ABOVE:
When Kenner decided to make a "gold" C-3PO action figure carrying case, it wanted to see how much packaging it needed to protect the finish in the shipping process. So it took about 100 of its black plastic Darth Vader carrying cases, vacuum metalized them in a gold finish, and shipped them to and from Kenner headquarters. This is a rare leftover from the test.

BELOW:
Sigma offered an extensive ceramic line made in Japan, including an R2-D2 string dispenser, Landspeeder soap dish, and Snowspeeder toothbrush holder. But few of the pieces were as elaborate as this sculpture of Luke Skywalker straddling his trusty Tauntaun. It's a teapot: Hold the Tauntaun by the tail and pour from his mouth.

LEFT:
Another "holy grail" for collectors is this Gamorrean Guard bank. Pictured on the back of other style banks from Adam Joseph, it was made only in limited quantities for the Canadian market. This one is a prototype.

109

RIGHT:
An MPC model kit of the Millennium Falcon, assembled and painted by a master craftsman at Industrial Light & Magic and used in a Lucasfilm display.

LEFT:
This Kenner Landspeeder is ready for the scene where Luke and Obi Wan Kenobi encounter a flock of Stormtroopers.

RIGHT:
Kenner sub-contracted this Speeder Bike pedal car to Huffy. The limited-production ride-on couldn't be purchased, only won in in-store and other contests

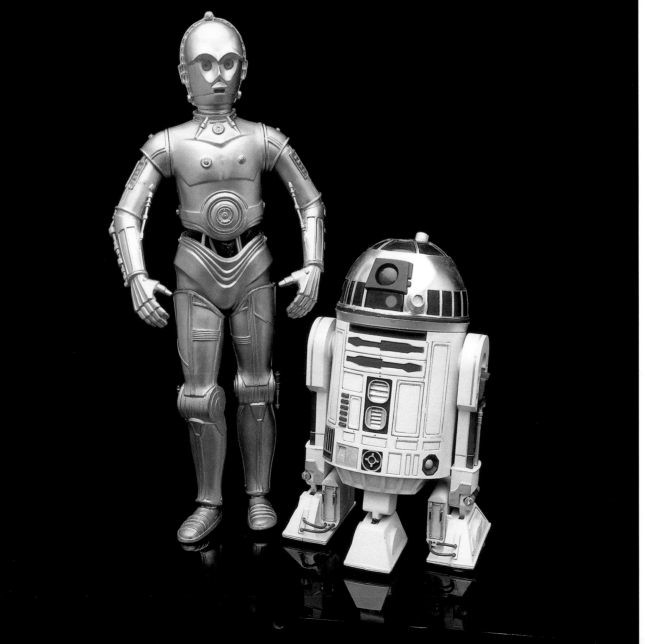

LEFT:
C-3PO and R2-D2 plastic model kits as assembled and painted by a model maker at Industrial Light & Magic.

Some fairly strange things were licensed in the early days. There was, for example, an act employing *Star Wars* characters at Circo Circo Americana in Mexico City; it had a six-week run and was used mainly to promote the film's debut there. A 20th Century Fox international representative let the Ann Street Brewery use C-3PO on a bus poster in Great Britain's Channel Islands. (Well, he did speak with a British accent.) But for every item approved, two dozen were rejected. Among the losers: a ballet featuring Darth Vader and a "space fantasy" disco that would look like a stylized version of the interior of the Millennium Falcon.

for teachers to use with slow learners. The Pendulum Press portfolio consisted of a special filmstrip and audio cassette version of the movie, along with a poster, five digest-sized comic books, and duplicating-machine sheets for *Star Wars* tests. ⚡ The huge success of *Star Wars* gave George Lucas the clout to renegotiate with Fox, and within a year he pulled the primary merchandising activities back into Lucasfilm. The film was opening all over the world, often in dubbed or subtitled versions, and the U.S. merchandising phenomenon was repeated in market after market—the first film to show such international appeal. In the United Kingdom alone, thirty-six manufacturers—only two of whom had ever before licensed a film—sold 136 different products. While some U.S. items were exported or made locally under license, much of the foreign merchandise was different. ⚡ "In Europe, many of the products tended to be at the lower end," Lippincott says. "Part of the consideration there was that kids—and their parents—had less money to spend." Less expensive doesn't have to mean shoddy. In Spain, for example, Ediciones Manantial sold a brightly colored R2-D2 rotating calendar and a C-3PO mobile made of thin cardboard. Italy's Edizioni Panini produced a colorful stamp album storybook for export all over Europe. England's Helix International made one of the few three-dimensional representations of the full Death Star: a tiny metal globe pencil sharpener for 35 pence. ⚡ *Star Wars* became an edible commodity in Europe and Asia —and eventually the U.S. In England alone there were ice lollies or popsicles, lemon chew bars, and molded marshmallows in the shapes of C-3PO, R2-D2, and Darth Vader. Italy had licorice twists. There were ice cream bars in Australia and Malaysia. And in Japan, a hungry film fan could buy chocolate or caramel candy,

RIGHT:
A colorful C-3PO mobile and an R2-D2 rotating calendar come from Ediciones Manantial of Spain.

OPPOSITE PAGE:
This brightly colored bagatelle, or mini-pinball game, is from Arco Falc in Italy.

BELOW:
A German CBS/Fox cardboard video store standee advertising the release of the Droids cartoon series on video cassettes.

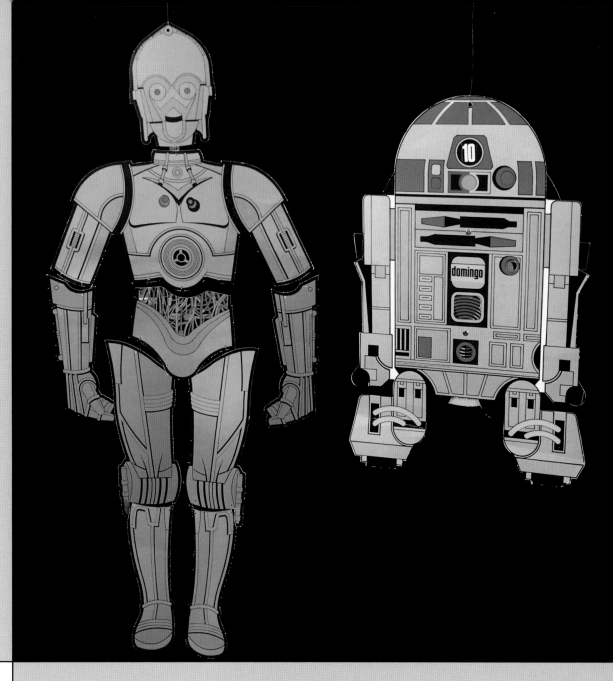

rice snacks, and dry bread sticks—all with small *Star Wars* premiums like Cracker Jack prizes. For *Jedi*, England's Bridge Farm Dairies offered *Star Wars* low-fat yogurt in eight varieties including the ever-popular Jabba the Hutt peach melba. ⚡ Despite Lucas's initial ban on sweetened cereal in the U.S. and his attempt to get American cereal makers to offer a truly nutritious sugar-free, low-preservative breakfast food for kids, he finally compromised on a less sweet cereal, C-3PO's by Kellogg's. There were also *Star Wars* cookies from Pepperidge Farm. Neither product was tasty enough to last very long, but both had great supermarket displays that collectors prize. ⚡ Lucasfilm's interest in promoting only healthful foods also led to an initial turndown in 1977 of a Canadian promotion featuring an offer for a *Star Wars* puzzle on labels for Libby's Alpha-Getti, a canned spaghetti product. Libby's

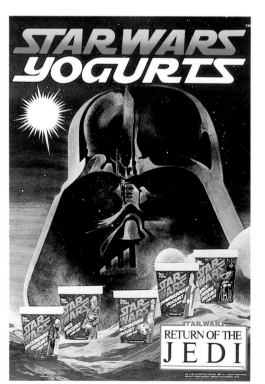

ABOVE:
Streets Ice Cream of Australia released its flavored ice treats in The Empire Strikes Back *boxes with three different sets of cut-outs on the back.*

LEFT:
British Star Wars *Dairy Time yogurt, from Bridge Farm Dairies, eventually came in eight delightful flavors, each picturing a hero or villain. Luke Skywalker was raspberry, Yoda was gooseberry, and Darth Vader was black cherry.*

ABOVE:
Tip Top of New Zealand gave away Ewok stickers with the purchase of its popsicles "with Jedi *jelly."*

Star Wars branded caramel and chocolate candy, bread sticks, and rice snacks came in colorful Japanese packaging. Most of the items came with a miniature figure or vehicle inside. There were dozens of different premiums.

Kellogg's C-3PO's cereal was purchased as much for the masks on the backs of the boxes as for the cereal inside. There were six masks in all to collect.

appealed, noting that its product was "a regular menu item for patients at The Hospital for Sick Children in Toronto." A compromise was struck. The promotion could proceed if Libby's also ran it on labels of an even more nutritious vegetable or tomato juice product. Fox controls overseas were looser. H. J. Heinz didn't have any problem with a British promotion for canned baked beans and sausage, and British kids could even get free *Star Wars* rub-downs by buying quarter-pound Wimpy burgers. ⚡ Promotional tie-ins became a major source of revenue and free advertising for the trilogy. *Star Wars* trading cards were stuck in more than sixty-five million loaves of Wonder Bread and General Mills promoted *Star Wars* cups, kites, cards, and stickers on twenty-five million cereal boxes. There were posters from Procter & Gamble; collectors' cards on six-pack trays of Hershey candy bars; and hats, placemats, and even a sweepstakes to win an in-home appearance by Darth Vader from the maker of Dixie cups. R2-D2 and C-3PO promoted childhood immunization campaigns in the U.S. and Australia and a savings campaign for the German post office. ⚡ But by far the most widespread and longest-lasting promotional tie-in was with the Coca-Cola Co. It was a great marriage between a company with an international presence and films that were cutting a swath across the world. In the U.S. there were

ABOVE:
The first and most stylish of many different sets of Star Wars *plastic soda cups all licensed by Coca-Cola Company. This 20-piece "limited collectors' edition" set was available at the Koolee chain.*

LEFT:
Millions of loaves of WonderBread were sold containing one of 16 collectors cards. The poster is part of a grocery-store display.

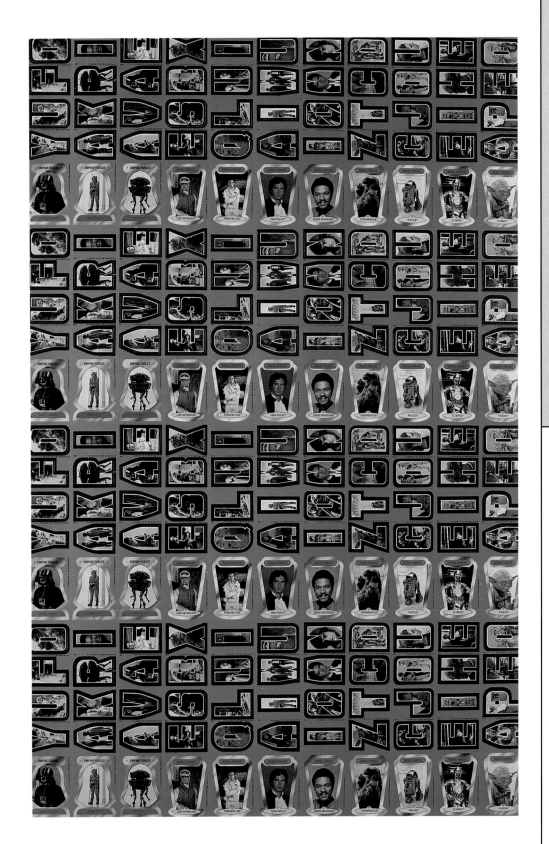

LEFT:

An uncut sheet of Topps stickers released along with trading cards for The Empire Strikes Back. *This set features printed photos inside every letter of the alphabet so that kids could personalize* Empire *signs.*

BELOW:

A grocery-store aisle display for Puffs tissues has scenes from The Empire Strikes Back. *The tissue boxes themselves also have scenes from the film and are sought by collectors—unopened if possible.*

ABOVE:
A "translite" plastic poster sheet from Burger King announcing its Star Wars *glasses premium.*

BELOW:
A few of the 50 bottle caps or crowns with Star Wars *photos offered by Coca-Cola Co. in Japan. Some of the caps were redeemable for premiums or prize money. There was also a flimsy plastic collectors' tray to hold the entire set.*

dozens of different plastic cups and glasses to collect from fast-food outlets and convenience stores. Coke also offered a flying disk, collectors' cards, and a stamp album in the U.S. In Asia, many of the Coke offers were tied to collecting bottle caps, or crowns, with photos of trilogy characters or vehicles inside. The biggest campaign was in Japan where there were fifty different caps and an R2-D2 radio with a Coca-Cola logo (only about 7,500 were made) that could be purchased during a two-month period for about $17 and ten Coke caps. In the U.S., there was a limited-edition Cobot, a radio-controlled R2-D2 look-alike, with the markings of a Coke can. ⚡ Although the foreign market for toys was dominated by Kenner licensed products nearly identical to those in the U.S., there were some notable exceptions. In England, Palitoy sold an ingenious and brightly colored chipboard Death

Three of the 12 premium glasses that Burger King and Coca-Cola issued—along with a purchase— for the Trilogy. Collectors also prize the in-store promotional posters and displays that accompanied the glasses.

Cobot, an R2-D2 clone, was made in Korea in limited numbers for Coca-Cola Co. collectors and only authorized by Lucasfilm after the fact. Accompanying paperwork notes a Lucasfilm design patent on the basic shape of R2-D2.

This rare limited-edition Japanese R2-D2 Coca-Cola radio, made by Fuji Electric, was a contest prize and a self-liquidating premium connected with collecting Coca-Cola bottle caps.

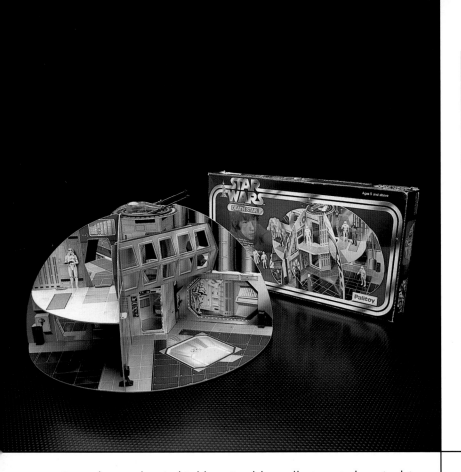

Great Britain's Waddingtons House of Games Ltd. was desperate to get out its series of boxed jigsaw puzzles, but Lucasfilm sent a stern telex in October 1977, forbidding use of one of the color photos Waddingtons planned to use. The scene was of Luke, Obi Wan, and the robots entering the Mos Eisley spaceport in Luke's landspeeder. But, Lucasfilm noted, the tires were visible on the landspeeder, which supposedly floated over the desert sands on a cushion of air. After promising to air-brush out the tires, Waddingtons got the permission it sought with one additional proviso: "You must remove the six telephone wires and the post in the background."

Star playset that is highly prized by collectors today. And in Japan, Takara came out with its own line of toys that were more detailed or technically oriented for the Japanese market. These include a sonic-control R2-D2 that "spits" plastic disks and another with a viewer in its stomach, showing seven different scenes from *Star Wars*; a large X-Wing Fighter that converts into dozens of other models; wooden model kits; tiny working die-cast figures and vehicles; and one of George Lucas's favorite toys, a two-inch-tall wind-up walking R2-D2. ⚡ In fact, Lucasfilm liked the walking R2-D2 so much that it constantly asked Kenner either to make one or to import Takara's. Kenner declined, presumably for fear of cutting into sales of its own R2-D2 action figure. Like even the best of marriages, that of Kenner and Lucasfilm had its occasional rough spots, but interviews with people at both com-

ABOVE LEFT:
A colorful, lithographed chipboard Death Star playset was sold only in England, France, and Canada. It is highly prized by collectors.

OPPOSITE PAGE,
CLOCKWISE FROM TOP:
C-3PO seems wise beyond his years wearing a Yoda cap from The Thinking Company. The droid head is a lighted fiberglass sculpture by Shigeru Hamano of Japan.

Shigeru Hamano also made this striking and fear-inspiring fiberglass mask of an Imperial TIE Fighter pilot.

A "garage kit," or unlicensed Japanese resin model of the bounty hunter Boba Fett, beautifully painted and detailed by Hiroshi Hamano.

Die-cast metal figures from Takara of Japan include an R2-D2 with a viewer and seven movie scenes in its chest, Darth Vader with a glow-in-the-dark lightsaber, and a most unlikely C-3PO that fires missiles from its chest.

A colorful bop bag by Takara. There it is known as a "punch-kick."

Takara made two different sized X-Wing Fighter toys. The larger one is convertible into five different vehicles for added play value.

CENTER:
This walking miniature R2-D2 windup from Takara was one of the favorite toys at Lucasfilm and ILM. The company itself ordered thousands of them for employees and friends of the company.

panies and a review of the voluminous correspondence between them indicate, on the whole, a remarkably harmonious relationship. ⚡ Maggie Young, who succeeded Charles Lippincott and headed the licensing and merchandising operations for nearly eight years, was the gatekeeper and the person charged with upholding quality. Kenner designers describe her as tough but fair as she held them to the highest possible standards. "Probably the scariest thing that George Lucas ever said to me," Young recalls, "was 'I put you in charge of the merchandising department, and if you do something that I don't like I'll let you know about it.' I was probably conservative to a fault in making judgments about whether or not something was done properly, whether a sculpting was good enough or a package was done in the right colors. After all, this was a series of films that everybody loved and seemed to have a proprietary interest in." ⚡ From the start, Lucasfilm made sure Kenner toys resembled the characters and vehicles from the films as closely as possible—a key to the line's long-term success. For example, it turned down the original plush Chewbacca made for Kenner by Canada's Regal Toys because the fur wasn't the right color and wasn't heavy enough, the face looked more like an orangutan, and there wasn't a bandolier-like shoulder shield. The toy was quickly fixed. ⚡ While Kenner was solicitous of Lucasfilm, it didn't agree to all of the company's suggestions. Among the suggested items it passed up were wooden blocks, hand puppets, doctor/nurse sets, a Leia fashion line for girls, and solar-powered toys. ⚡ The main bone of contention over the years was plush or stuffed toys. George Lucas himself frequently expressed interest in more such toys, but Kenner had little experience in producing them, wouldn't sublicense them, and had trou-

ble making its prototypes "soft and cuddly" as Lucasfilm desired. ⚡ The issue came to a head over the Ewoks. Lucas was convinced that, properly done, plush toys of these primitive, furry creatures could become almost as popular as teddy bears. But it was difficult making these fierce warriors soft and cuddly, and also making them look different enough to give them individual personalities. The prototypes went back and forth between Cincinnati and Skywalker Ranch, undergoing constant change. In the end, sales were disappointing. ⚡ Even after the tremendous success of *Star Wars*, trying to license *The Empire Strikes Back* "was like running into a brick wall," Young says. "People looked at the first film as a fluke, and sequels hadn't been very successful up until then." By the time *Return of the Jedi* was released in 1983, however, the licensing industry had finally caught on to what Lucasfilm was doing, and manufacturers were more eager to sign on. ⚡ Besides the licensed products, there were other, non-mass-produced items that *Star Wars* fans seek for their collections. These include variously sized posters and lobby cards made for movie theaters, along with press books and press kits. In the U.S. alone, the trilogy produced an astonishing twenty-three different one-sheets, the standard twenty-seven by forty-one-inch posters that cinemas hang in outdoor frames. Add distinctive foreign posters

TOP, FROM LEFT TO RIGHT:

The Star Wars *Concert was a one-night affair at the Hollywood Bowl, where this limited-run poster—with art by John Alvin—was sold. It's one of the rarest and most highly prized* Star Wars *posters today with a price well above $500.*

National Public Radio had two huge hits when it serialized expanded versions of Star Wars *and* Empire *in a total of 23 music and sound-effects filled episodes. There were plans to tackle* Jedi, *but funds weren't available.*

Perhaps the most unusual of the hundreds of foreign theatrical Trilogy posters are these two from Poland: A hand-tinted C-3PO in what looks like a blizzard for Star Wars *and an exploding Darth Vader head for* Jedi *by W. Dybowski.*

U.S.A.

U.S.A.

BOTTOM, FROM LEFT TO RIGHT:

This Italian poster for Star Wars *uses unique cartoon-style art.*

Here's an early concept for a theatrical poster by production illustrator Ralph McQuarrie and actual posters from Hong Kong and Israel.

Talk about a hot poster! This unusual image was done by noted Japanese artist Noriyoshi Ohrai for limited-edition sale.

ITALY

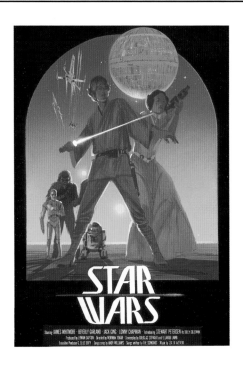

U.S.A.

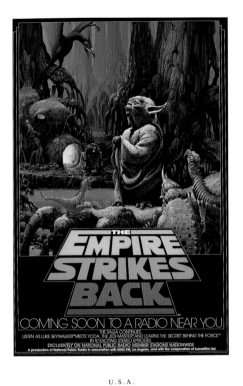

U.S.A.

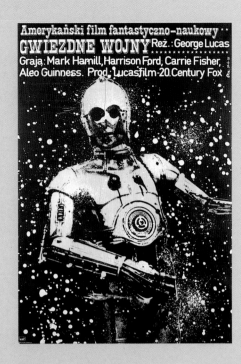

POLAND

POLAND

HONG KONG

ISRAEL

JAPAN

from Israel to Hong Kong to Poland, plus advertising sheets for products around the world, and there are well over 750 different posters. ⚡ There are also limited-edition promotional items, including a Lucite star that Lucas gave to cast and crew at an early *Star Wars* screening, brass paperweights with the films' names, and even a "passport" used to admit VIPs to the set of *The Empire Strikes Back* in England. Some collectors seek original art from the posters or books, and even some pieces of props or costumes have made it into the collecting world. Lucasfilm has occasionally given away things such as a piece of the Death Star in a fan club sweepstakes, an original script, or a C-3PO hand to be auctioned off for charity (one sold for $5,000). ⚡ By 1985, the youngsters who had driven the *Star Wars* frenzy were ready to move on to something new. "There's a natural life cycle to properties with strong kid

Before George Lucas decided that a Jedi doesn't seek "revenge," a number of items like this paperweight were developed.

STAR·WARS
REVENGE OF THE
JEDI

appeal," notes Howard Roffman, the LucasArts Entertainment Company vice-president, licensing. "Even classics like Mickey Mouse go through cycles. The kids who were enamored of *Star Wars*, and their younger brothers and sisters, started to grow out of it and there weren't any new films to attract the next group." ⚡ But the *Star Wars* phenomenon is far from dead; it's just resting in the public's subconscious. There still are events such as the tenth anniversary celebration of *Star Wars*, a 1987 fan convention that got huge media coverage. There are four *Star Tours* rides at Disney theme parks on three continents. A collectors' silver and gold coin set released in 1988 has already shot up in value. Coin dealers say there were only fourteen complete sets of all twenty-four coins minted (although one coin sold fifteen-thousand copies). A set is worth $20,000 to $25,000, dealers estimate. ⚡ Collectors also can buy hand-painted cels from the *Ewoks* and *Droids* TV cartoon series. But by far the biggest indication that a galaxy of fans are still enamored of the *Star Wars* universe was the tremendous success in the summer of 1991 of a new novel, *Heir to the Empire*, set in a familiar galaxy five years after the destruction of the Death Star. The book, by well-known science fiction writer Timothy Zahn, soared to number one on the national fiction bestseller list and stayed on the list for months. It was the first of a three-book cycle by Zahn and launched an ambitious new publishing program using *Star Wars* characters in such things as children's books and comics. ⚡ Now, it's George Lucas's move. In the past, he talked about nine films, but later indicated there wouldn't be any more after *Jedi*. ⚡ Seated in his large, comfortable office at Skywalker Ranch, Lucas says he's still on track to carry out his

Rarities Mint produced six different coin designs to commemorate the 10th Anniversary of Star Wars.

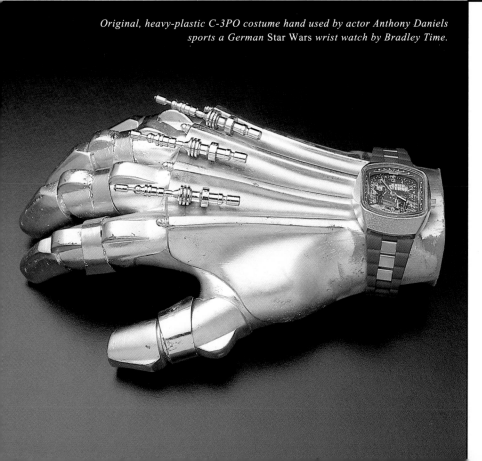

Original, heavy-plastic C-3PO costume hand used by actor Anthony Daniels sports a German Star Wars *wrist watch by Bradley Time.*

1990 announcement that he'll probably make the next three *Star Wars* films for release starting in 1997. His plan is to try to film them all together, but release them a year or so apart. The films will start the saga, and be the first three chapters, with the existing films becoming either the center or the end of the epic. ⚡ "I think I've got a really good story for the next films," Lucas reflects, "and I'd love to tell it. And I guess I've got the creative urge at least to complete the first part of the saga. While some people will have expectations that will be impossible to fulfill, there will be a whole new generation of moviegoers out there. It's going to be like starting all over again."

S O U R C E S

The vast majority of this book comes from nearly 40 hours of taped interviews with two dozen people who work, or worked, for Lucasfilm, Industrial Light & Magic, Kenner Products, and 20th Century Fox Film. These interviews were backed up with an extensive search through relevant files and archives at Skywalker Ranch—including the photo library and prop archives. That material was supplemented with information gleaned from the author's extensive collection of *Star Wars* memorabilia, photos, clippings, and merchandise. New photos are of items from the author's collection or from the Kenner archives. Additional photos are from the Lucasfilm or ILM archives. In addition, there were several books and magazine articles that were particularly helpful. Foremost among these was *Skywalking: The Life and Films of George Lucas,* by Dale Pollock (New York: Harmony Books, 1983), which was a major resource in confirming dates and places and providing additional background from the time of the filming of *Star Wars.* Each chapter begins with an excerpt of dialog from one of the three *Star Wars* films. In this case, the quotations were taken from a digest series of *Screenplay* books published in Japan in 1990 and 1991 by Four-In Creative Products Corp.; they are published to help teach English. Two series of books published by Ballantine in conjunction with the release of each of the films also were used for reference. They were *The Art of Star Wars, The Art of The Empire Strikes Back* and *The Art of Return of the Jedi;* and *The Star Wars Sketchbook, The Empire Strikes Back Sketchbook* and *Return of the Jedi Sketchbook.* Two magazines were especially useful. They were *Cinefex,* the August and December 1980 issues; and *American Cinematographer,* the issues of July 1977, June 1980, and June 1983.

I N D E X

"Bleep blit bloop blot."

"Yes, R2, it seems that

our adventure is at an end...

or is that a new beginning

I see just up ahead?"